THE BOTTOM OF
THE HARBOR

THE BOTTOM OF
THE HARBOR

Joseph Mitchell

FOREWORD BY LUC SANTE

PANTHEON BOOKS
NEW YORK

All rights reserved. Published in the United States by
Pantheon Books, a division of Random House, Inc., New York,
and in Canada by Random House of Canada Limited, Toronto.

Pantheon Books and colophon are registered trademarks of
Random House, Inc.

Originally published in slightly different form by Little, Brown
in 1959. All of the pieces in this work were subsequently
collected in *Up in the Old Hotel* (Pantheon, 1992).

Library of Congress Cataloging-in-Publication Data
Mitchell, Joseph, 1908–1996
The bottom of the harbor / Joseph Mitchell ; foreword by
Luc Sante.—1st rev. ed.
p.   cm.
"Originally published in slightly different form by Little,
Brown in 1959"—T.p. verso.
ISBN 978-0-375-71486-3
1. New York (N.Y.)—Social life and customs.   2. Harbors—
New York (State)—New York.   3. Waterfronts—New York
(State)—New York.   I. Title.
F128.63.M5 2008
974.7′1—dc22   2008009494

www.pantheonbooks.com

Printed in the United States of America

First Revised Edition
2   4   6   8   9   7   5   3   1

TO

NORA AND ELIZABETH MITCHELL

Contents

Foreword

When the stories in this book were first published, between 1944 and 1959, the harbor of New York was at its peak. The harbor and its many trades were an integral part of the city's daily fabric, and as such they passed largely unnoticed by most citizens. That is the usual fate of tradition, and it follows that hardly anyone foresaw its eclipse. Within a couple of decades of the book's publication the better part of its subject matter had passed into history. Joseph Mitchell may not have thought that he was writing the harbor's epitaph, but he was certainly aware of its fragility, all appearances to the contrary.

The transience of so many urban commonplaces that in their time seemed enduring to the point of immutability—indeed, to the point where they escaped conscious notice—was a preoccupation of Mitchell's. For all that he had come to New York from rural North Carolina, he had absorbed the city's fabric, both in its course over time and its daily apparatus, and he appreciated its changes and mourned its losses as few others did. When the neighborhood that contained Washington Market—the great produce exchange that had ruled the city's diet since the eighteenth century—was felled in the name of progress in the 1960s, he went around collecting bits of the structures: small fixtures that, fittingly, had gone unnoticed in their years of use but that he pressed into service as memorial markers.

But Mitchell should not be mistaken for a gravedigger. He was drawn to the harbor first of all because he was interested in people, in process, in specialized skills, in accreted time, in individual reckonings with tradition, in the annexes and alcoves and side rooms left out of the broader historical account. And he was drawn there by his senses—by the sound of names and the look of things and the odor of the sea and the taste of its fruits. In his pieces he walks through stories that bring together many of these fascinations; he watches people work, listens to their stories, savors them in the moment and at the same time regards them *sub specie aeternitatis*. An empty hotel above a bustling fish-market restaurant; the polluted remains of the once-flourishing oyster and clam beds in the harbor; the lives and exploits of the rats that come to the city aboard ships; the gentle decline of what began as a settlement of freed slaves in Staten Island; the labor of the captain of the biggest fishing fleet in the region; the unique practices of the shad fishermen at the foot of the Palisades in New Jersey—all of these are dense with color, flavor, humor, anecdotes, museum-quality details, and intimations of mortality.

Mitchell was a man of many interests, a brooder, a cataloger, an inveterate walker, and clearly one of the greatest listeners who ever lived. Just as the term "journalist" seems like a reductive label for his trade, so "interview" is utterly inadequate as a description of his chief working tool. He didn't use a recording device (not that such things were even available then) and didn't even ask many questions. By all accounts, he had a way of intently listening that by itself caused his subjects to keep talking. And then he reproduced what he had heard, with respect for his subjects and mindful of their rhythms of speech, but otherwise unconstrained by the slavish fidelity to minutiae that fact-checkers and legal counsel insist upon nowadays—and in the process turned all of his subjects into plain-spoken masters of American prose.

Mitchell's verbal artistry is subtle, and it can be nearly invisible to the casual reader. This was by design. Few writers have been as self-effacing as Mitchell, whose reticence is one of the most striking contrasts between him and A. J. Liebling—his friend, *New Yorker* colleague, and fellow enthusiast of New

York City, plain cooking, and popular speech—who was the cheerful rotund extrovert to Mitchell's thin melancholy introvert. Its subtlety was also a function of its deeply American aesthetic. Mitchell, whose favorite book was *Ulysses,* devised an equivalent in prose to the rigorous and deceptive simplicity of Walker Evans's photographs and Charles Sheeler's paintings. Mitchell's favorite device was the list, and his favorite conjunction was "and": "dust and lint and grit and slut's wool"; "mussels and mud shrimp and conchs and crabs and sea worms and sea plants"; "old anchors and worm wheels and buoys and bollards and propellors." Setting these objects side by side in a row has an effect that is both as plain as Shaker furniture and as expansive as a cinematic tracking shot. It also seems as functional as clapboard siding, although it is worth noting that across the page from the last of these cited lists, Mitchell records the message of a pulsating electric sign: "'SPRY FOR BAKING,' 'SPRY FOR BAKING,' 'SPRY FOR BAKING.'" There is nothing accidental about Mitchell's rhythms.

In his most personal and revealing piece of writing, the introduction to the omnibus collection *Up in the Old Hotel* (1992), Mitchell mentions his affinity for the works of the Mexican graphic artist José Guadalupe Posada, famous for hilarious catastrophes and smartly turned-out antic skeletons, the salient feature being gallows humor. That aspect of his work is spelled out in this book's epigraph: "The worms crawl in, / The worms crawl out . . ." Had Mitchell lived in the Elizabethan era he might have been considered an antiquarian, like another kindred spirit, Robert Burton, the brooding and indefatigably list-making author of *The Anatomy of Melancholy*. Like Burton, Mitchell meditates on graveyards and ruins, as well as doomed occupations and superannuated traditions, but what might at first appear to be a morbid streak turns out to be a homeopathic practice. Mitchell knew that an appreciation of death is necessary for an understanding of the regenerative cycle, the turning of the world. He could savor the perhaps galling fact that so many aspects of the world are taken for granted and only become truly visible at their twilight. The more he looked at the ends of things, the sharper his appetite for life, for sensual pleasures and creative disorder. This book of ostensibly journalistic feature stories turns out to hold at its core some of the fundamental questions of existence.

Luc Sante

The worms crawl in,
The worms crawl out.
They eat your guts
And spit them out . . .

—Children's Song

Author's Note

The stories in this book first appeared in *The New Yorker,* but not in the order in which they are now arranged. The first story, "Up in the Old Hotel," came out in the magazine under the title of "The Cave" in the issue of June 28, 1952; the second, "The Bottom of the Harbor," came out in the issue of January 6, 1951; the third, "The Rats on the Waterfront," came out under the title of "Thirty-two Rats from Casablanca," in the issue of April 29, 1944; the fourth, "Mr. Hunter's Grave," came out in the issue of September 22, 1956; the fifth, "Dragger Captain," came out in two parts in the issues of January 4 and January 11, 1947; and the sixth, "The Rivermen," came out in the issue of April 4, 1959.

The people in all of the stories are connected in one way or another with the waterfront of New York City.

THE BOTTOM OF
THE HARBOR

Up in the Old Hotel

Every now and then, seeking to rid my mind of
thoughts of death and doom, I get up early and go
down to Fulton Fish Market. I usually arrive around
five-thirty, and take a walk through the two huge
open-fronted market sheds, the Old Market and the
New Market, whose fronts rest on South Street and
whose backs rest on piles in the East River. At that
time, a little while before the trading begins, the
stands in the sheds are heaped high and spilling over
with forty to sixty kinds of finfish and shellfish from
the East Coast, the West Coast, the Gulf Coast, and
half a dozen foreign countries. The smoky riverbank
dawn, the racket the fishmongers make, the seaweedy smell, and the sight of this plentifulness
always give me a feeling of well-being, and sometimes they elate me. I wander among the stands for
an hour or so. Then I go into a cheerful market

restaurant named Sloppy Louie's and eat a big, inexpensive, invigorating breakfast—a kippered herring and scrambled eggs, or a shad-roe omelet, or split sea scallops and bacon, or some other breakfast specialty of the place.

Sloppy Louie's occupies the ground floor of an old building at 92 South Street, diagonally across the street from the sheds. This building faces the river and looks out on the slip between the Fulton Street fish pier and the Old Porto Rico Line dock. It is six floors high, and it has two windows to the floor. Like the majority of the older buildings in the market district, it is made of hand-molded Hudson River brick, a rosy-pink and relatively narrow kind that used to be turned out in Haverstraw and other kiln towns on the Hudson and sent down to the city in barges. It has an ornamented tin cornice and a slate-covered mansard roof. It is one of those handsome, symmetrical old East River waterfront buildings that have been allowed to dilapidate. The windows of its four upper floors have been boarded over for many years, a rain pipe that runs down the front of it is riddled with rust holes, and there are gaps here and there on its mansard where slates have slipped off. In the afternoons, after two or three, when the trading is over and the stands begin to close, some of the slimy, overfed gulls that scavenge in the market roost along its cornice, hunched up and gazing downward.

4

I have been going to Sloppy Louie's for nine or ten years, and the proprietor and I are old friends. His name is Louis Morino, and he is a contemplative and generous and worldly-wise man in his middle sixties. Louie is a North Italian. He was born in Recco, a fishing and bathing-beach village thirteen miles southeast of Genoa, on the Eastern Riviera. Recco is ancient; it dates back to the third century. Families in Genoa and Milan and Turin own villas in and around it, and go there in the summer. Some seasons, a few English and Americans show up. According to a row of colored-postcard views of it Scotch-taped to a mirror on the wall in back of Louie's cash register, it is a village of steep streets and tall, square, whitewashed stone houses. The fronts of the houses are decorated with stenciled designs— madonnas, angels, flowers, fruit, and fish. The fish design is believed to protect against the evil eye and appears most often over doors and windows. Big, lush fig bushes grow in almost every yard. In the center of the village is an open-air market where fishermen and farmers sell their produce off plank-and-sawhorse counters. Louie's father was a fisherman. His name was Giuseppe Morino, and he was called, in Genoese dialect, Beppe du Russu, or Joe the Redhead. "My family was one of the old fishing families in Recco that the priest used to tell us had been fishing along that coast since Roman times," Louie says. "We lived on a street named the Vico Saporito that was paved with broken-up sea shells and wound in and out and led down to the water. My father did a kind of fishing that's called haul-seining over here, and he set lobster traps and jigged for squid and bobbed for octopuses. When the weather was right, he used to row out to an underwater cave he knew about and anchor over it and take a bob consisting of a long line with scraps of raw meat hung from it every foot or so and a stone on the end of it and drop it in the mouth of the cave, and the octopuses would shoot up out of the dark down there and swallow the meat scraps and that would hold them, and then my father would draw the bob up slow and steady and pull the octopuses loose from the meat scraps one by one and toss them in a tub in the boat. He'd bob up enough octopuses in a couple of hours to glut the market in Recco. This cave was full of octopuses; it was choked with them. He had found it, and he had the rights to it. The other fishermen didn't go near it; they called it Beppe du Russu's cave. In addition to fishing, he kept a rickety old bathhouse on the beach for the summer people. It stood on stilts, and I judge it had fifty to sixty rooms. We called it the Bagni Margherita. My mother ran a little buffet in connection with it."

Louie left Recco in 1905, when he was close to eighteen. "I loved my family," he says, "and it tore me in two to leave, but I have five brothers and two sisters, and all my brothers were younger than me, and there were already too many fishermen in Recco, and the bathhouse brought in just so much, and I had a persisting fear there might not be enough at home to go around in time to come, so I got passage from Genoa to New York scrubbing pots in the galley of a steamship and went straight from the dock to a chophouse on East 138th Street in the Bronx that was operated by a man named Capurro who came from Recco. Capurro knew my father when they both were boys." Capurro gave Louie a job washing dishes and taught him how to wait on tables. He stayed there two years. For the next twenty-three years, he worked as a waiter in restaurants all over Manhattan and Brooklyn. He has forgotten how many he worked in; he can recall the names of thirteen. Most of them were medium-size restaurants of the Steaks-&-Chops, We-Specialize-in-Seafood, Tables-for-Ladies type. In the winter of 1930, he decided to risk his savings and become his own boss. "At that time," he says, "the stock-market crash had shook everything up and the depression was setting in, and I knew of several restaurants in midtown that could be bought at a bargain—lease, furnishings, and good will. All were up-to-date places. Then I ran into a waiter I used to work with and he told me about this old run-down restaurant in an old run-down building in the fish market that was for sale, and I went and saw it, and I took it. The reason I did, Fulton Fish Market reminds me of Recco. There's a world of difference between them. At the same time, they're very much alike—the fish smell, the general gone-to-pot look, the trading that goes on in the streets, the roofs over the sidewalks, the cats in corners gnawing on fish heads, the gulls in the gutters, the way everybody's on to everybody else, the quarreling and the arguing. There's a boss fishmonger down here, a spry old hardheaded Italian man who's got a million dollars in the bank and dresses like he's on relief and walks up and down the fish pier snatching fish out of barrels by their heads or their tails and weighing them in his hands and figuring out in his mind to a fraction of a fraction how much they're worth and shouting and singing and enjoying life, and the face on him, the way he conducts himself, he reminds me so much of my father that sometimes, when I see him, it puts me in a good humor, and sometimes it breaks my heart."

Louie is five feet six, and stocky. He has an owl-like face—his nose is hooked, his eyebrows are tufted, and his eyes are large and brown and observant. He is white-haired. His complexion is reddish, and his face and the backs of his hands are speckled with freckles and liver spots. He wears glasses with flesh-colored frames. He is bandy-legged, and he carries his left shoulder lower than his right and walks with a shuffling, hipshot, head-up, old-waiter's walk. He dresses neatly. He has his suits made by a high-priced tailor in the insurance district, which adjoins the fish-market district. Starting work in the morning, he always puts on a fresh apron and a fresh brown linen jacket. He keeps a napkin folded over his left arm even when he is standing behind the cash register. He is a proud man, and somewhat stiff and formal by nature, but he unbends easily and he has great curiosity and he knows how to get along with people. During rush hours, he jokes and laughs with his customers and recommends his daily specials in extravagant terms and listens to fish-market gossip and passes it on; afterward, in repose, having a cup of coffee by himself at a table in the rear, he is grave.

Louie is a widower. His wife, Mrs. Victoria Piazza Morino, came from a village named Ruta that is only two and a half miles from Recco, but he first became acquainted with her in Brooklyn. They were married in 1928, and he was deeply devoted to her. She died in 1949. He has two daughters—Jacqueline, who is twenty-two and was recently graduated from the Mills College of Education, a school for nursery, kindergarten, and primary teachers on lower Fifth Avenue, and Lois, who is seventeen and was recently graduated from Fontbonne Hall, a high school on Shore Road in Brooklyn that is operated by the Sisters of St. Joseph. They are smart, bright, slim, vivid, dark-eyed girls. Louie has to be on hand in his restaurant in the early morning, and he usually gets up between four and five, but before leaving home he always squeezes orange juice and puts coffee on the stove for his daughters. Most days, he gets home before they do and cooks dinner.

Louie owns his home, a two-story brick house on a maple-bordered street in the predominantly Norwegian part of the Bay Ridge neighborhood in Brooklyn. There is a saying in Recco that people and fig bushes do best close to salt water; Louie's home is only a few blocks from the Narrows, and fifteen years ago he ordered three tiny fig bushes from a nursery in Virginia and set them out in his back yard, and they have flourished. In the late fall, he wraps an accumulation of worn-out suits and dresses and sweaters and sheets and blankets around their trunks and limbs. "All winter," he says, "when I look out the back window, it looks like I got three mummies stood up out there." At the first sign of spring, he takes the wrappings off. The bushes begin to bear the middle of July and bear abundantly during August. One bush bears small white figs, and the others bear plump black figs that split their skins down one side as they ripen and gape open and show their pink and violet flesh. Louie likes to gather the figs around dusk, when they are still warm from the heat of the day. Sometimes, bending beside a bush, he plunges his face into the leaves and breathes in the musky smell of the ripening figs, a smell that fills his mind with memories of Recco in midsummer.

Louie doesn't think much of the name of his restaurant. It is an old restaurant with old furnishings that has had a succession of proprietors and a succession of names. Under the proprietor preceding Louie, John Barbagelata, it was named the Fulton Restaurant, and was sometimes called Sloppy John's. When Louie took it over, he changed the name to Louie's Restaurant. One of the fishmongers promptly started calling it Sloppy Louie's, and Louie made a mistake and remonstrated with him. He remonstrated with him on several occasions. As soon as the people in the market caught on to the fact that the name offended Louie, naturally most of them began using it. They got in the habit of using it. Louie brooded about the matter off and on for over three years, and then had a new swinging signboard erected above his door with SLOPPY LOUIE's RESTAURANT on it in big red letters. He even changed his listing in the telephone book. "I couldn't beat them," he says, "so I joined them."

Sloppy Louie's is small and busy. It can seat eighty, and it crowds up and thins out six or seven times a day. It opens at five in the morning and closes at eight-thirty in the evening. It has a double door in front with a show window on each side. In one window are three sailing-ship models in whiskey bottles, a giant lobster claw with eyes and a mouth painted on it, a bulky oyster shell, and a small skull. Beside the shell is a card on which Louie has neatly written, "Shell of an Oyster dredged from the bottom of Great South Bay. Weighed two and a quarter pounds. Estimated to be fifteen years old. Said to be largest ever dredged in G.S.B." Beside the skull is a similar card, which says, "This is the skull of a Porpoise taken by a dragger off Long Beach, Long Island." In the other window is an old pie cupboard with glass sides. To the left, as you enter, is a combined cigar showcase and cashier's desk, and an iron safe with a cash register on top of it. There are mirrors all around the walls. Four lamps and three electric fans with wooden blades that resemble propellers hang from the stamped-tin ceiling. The tables in Louie's are communal, and there are exactly one dozen; six jut out from the wall on one side of the room and six jut out from the wall on the other side, and a broad aisle divides them. They are long tables, and solid and old and plain and built to last. They are made of black walnut; Louie once repaired a leg on one, and said it was like driving a nail in iron. Their tops have been seasoned by drippings and spillings from thousands upon thousands of platters of broiled fish, and their edges have been scratched and scarred by the hatchets and bale hooks that hang from frogs on fishmongers' belts. They are identical in size; some seat six, and some have a chair on the aisle end and seat seven. At the back of the room, hiding the door to the kitchen, is a huge floor mirror on which, each morning, using a piece of moistened chalk, Louie writes the menu for the day. It is sometimes a lengthy menu. A good many dishes are served in Louie's that are rarely served in other restaurants. One day, interspersed among the staple seafood-restaurant dishes, Louie listed cod cheeks, salmon cheeks, cod tongues, sturgeon liver, blue-shark steak, tuna steak, squid stew, and five kinds of roe—shad roe, cod roe, mackerel roe, herring roe, and yellow-pike roe. Cheeks are delectable morsels of flesh that are found in the heads of some species of fish, one on each side, inset in bone and cartilage. The men who dress fish in the fillet houses in the market cut out a few quarts of cheeks whenever they have the time to spare and sell them to Louie. Small shipments of them come down occasionally from the Boston Fish Pier, and the fishmongers, thinking of their own gullets, let Louie buy most of them. The fishmongers use Louie's as a testing kitchen. When anything unusual is shipped to the market, it is taken to Louie's and tried out. In the course of a year, Louie's undoubtedly serves a wider variety of seafood than any other restaurant in the country.

.   .   .

When I go to Sloppy Louie's for breakfast, I always
try to get a chair at one of the tables up front, and
Louie generally comes out from behind the cash register and tells me what is best to order. Some mornings, if there is a lull in the breakfast rush, he draws
himself a cup of coffee and sits down with me. One
morning a while back, he sat down, and I asked him
how things were going, and he said he couldn't complain, he had about as much business as he could handle. "My breakfast trade still consists almost entirely
of fishmongers and fish buyers," he said, "but my
lunch trade has undergone a change. The last few
years, a good many people in the districts up above
the market have taken to walking down here occasionally for lunch—people from the insurance district, the financial district, and the coffee-roasting
district. Some days, from noon to three, they outnumber the fishmongers. I hadn't realized myself
how great a change had taken place until just the
other day I happened to notice the mixed-up nature
of a group of people sitting around one table. They
were talking back and forth, the way people do in
here that never even saw each other before, and passing the ketchup, and I'll tell you who they were.
Sitting on one side was an insurance broker from
Maiden Lane, and next to him was a fishmonger
named Mr. Frank Wilkisson who's a member of a

family that's had a stand in the Old Market three generations, and next to him was a young Southerner that you're doing good if you understand half what he says who drives one of those tremendous big refrigerator trucks that they call reefers and hits the market every four or five days with a load of shrimp from little shrimp ports in Florida and Georgia. Sitting on the other side was a lady who holds a responsible position in Continental Casualty up on William Street and comes in here for bouillabaisse, only we call it *ciuppin di pesce* and cook it the way it's cooked fishing-family style back in Recco, and next to her was an old gentleman who works in J. P. Morgan & Company's banking house and you'd think he'd order something expensive like pompano but he always orders cod cheeks and if we're out of that he orders cod roe and if we're out of that he orders broiled cod and God knows we're never out of that, and next to him was one of the bosses in Mooney's coffee-roasting plant at Fulton and Front. And sitting at the aisle end of the table was a man known all over as Cowhide Charlie who goes to slaughterhouses and buys green cowhides and sells them to fishing-boat captains to rig to the undersides of their drag nets to keep them from getting bottom-chafed and rock-cut and he's always bragging that right this very minute his hides are rubbing the bottom of every fishing bank from Nantucket Shoals to the Virginia Capes."

Louie said that some days, particularly Fridays, the place is jammed around one o'clock and late-comers crowd together just inside the door and stand and wait and stare, and he said that this gets on his nerves. He said he had come to the conclusion that he would have to go ahead and put in some tables on the second floor.

"I would've done it long ago," he said, "except I need the second floor for other things. This building doesn't have a cellar. South Street is old filled-in river swamp, and the cellars along here, what few there are, the East River leaks into them every high tide. The second floor is my cellar. I store supplies up there, and I keep my Deepfreeze up there, and the waiters change their clothes up there. I don't know what I'll do without it, only I got to make room someway."

"That ought to be easy," I said. "You've got four empty floors up above."

"You mean those boarded-up floors," Louie said. He hesitated a moment. "Didn't I ever tell you about the upstairs in here?" he asked. "Didn't I ever tell you about those boarded-up floors?"

"No," I said.

"They aren't empty," he said

"What's in them?" I asked.

"I don't know," he said. "I've heard this and I've heard that, but I don't know. I wish to God I did know. I've wondered about it enough. I've rented this building twenty-two years, and I've never been above the second floor. The reason being, that's as far as the stairs go. After that, you have to get in a queer old elevator and pull yourself up. It's an old-fashioned hand-power elevator, what they used to call a rope-pull. I wouldn't be surprised it's the last of its kind in the city. I don't understand the machinery of it, the balancing weights and the cables and all that, but the way it's operated, there's a big iron wheel at the top of the shaft and the wheel's got a groove in it, and there's a rope that hangs down one side of the cage to go up, and you pull on the part that hangs down the other side to go down. Like a dumbwaiter. It used to run from the ground floor to the top, but a long time ago some tenant must've decided he didn't have any further use for it and wanted it out of the way, so he had the shaft removed from the ground floor and the second floor. He had it cut off at the second-floor ceiling. In other words, the way it is now, the bottom of the shaft is level with the second-floor ceiling—the floor of the elevator cage acts as part of the ceiling. To get in the elevator, you have to climb a ladder that leads to a trap door that's cut in the floor of the cage. It's a big, roomy cage, bigger than the ones nowadays, but it doesn't have a roof on it—just this wooden floor and some iron-framework sides. I go up the ladder sometimes and push up the trap door and put my head and shoulders inside the cage and shine a flashlight up the shaft, but that's as far as I go. Oh, Jesus, it's dark and dusty in there. The cage is all furry with dust and there's mold and mildew on the walls of the shaft and the air is dead.

"The first day I came here, I wanted to get right in the elevator and go up to the upper floors and rummage around up there, see what I could see, but the man who rented the building ahead of me was with me, showing me over the place, and he warned me not to. He didn't trust the elevator. He said you couldn't pay him to get in it. 'Don't meddle with that thing,' he said. 'It's a rattlesnake. The rope might break, or that big iron wheel up at the top of the shaft that's eaten up with rust and hasn't been oiled for a generation might work loose and drop on your head.' Consequently, I've never even given the rope a pull. To pull the rope, you got to get inside the cage and stand up. You can't reach it otherwise. I've been tempted to many a time. It's a thick hemp rope. It's as thick as a hawser. It might be rotten, but it certainly looks strong. The way the cage is sitting now, I figure it'd only take a couple of pulls, a couple of turns of the wheel, and you'd be far enough up to where you could swing the cage door open and step out on the third floor. You can't open the cage door now; you got to draw the cage up just a little. A matter of inches. I reached into the cage once and tried to poke the door open with a boat hook I borrowed off one of the fishing boats, but it wouldn't budge. It's a highly irritating situation to me. I'd just like to know for certain what's up there. A year goes by sometimes and I hardly think about it, and then I get to wondering, and it has a tendency to prey on my mind. An old-timer in the market once told me that many years ago a fishmonger down here got a bug in his head and invented a patented returnable zinc-lined fish box for shipping fish on ice and had hundreds of them built, sunk everything he had in them, and they didn't catch on, and finally he got permission to store them up on the third and fourth floors of this building until he could come to some conclusion what to do with them. This was back before they tinkered with the elevator. Only he never came to any conclusion, and by and by he died. The old-timer said it was his belief the fish boxes are still up there. The man who rented the building ahead of me, he had a different story. He was never above the second floor either, but he told me that one of the men who rented it ahead of him told him it was his understanding there was a lot of miscellaneous old hotel junk stored up there—beds and bureaus, pitchers and bowls, chamber pots, mirrors, brass spittoons, odds and ends, old hotel registers that the rats chew on to get paper to line their nests with, God knows what all. That's what he said. I don't know. I've made quite a study of this building for one reason and another, and I've took all kinds of pains tracking things down, but there's a lot about it I still don't know. I do know there was a hotel in here years back. I know that beyond all doubt. It was one of those old steamship hotels that used to face the docks all along South Street."

"Why don't you get a mechanic to inspect the elevator?" I asked. "It might be perfectly safe."

"That would cost money," Louie said. "I'm curious, but I'm not that curious. To tell you the truth, I just don't want to get in that cage by myself. I got a feeling about it, and that's the fact of the matter. It makes me uneasy—all closed in, and all that furry dust. It makes me think of a coffin, the inside of a coffin. Either that or a cave, the mouth of a cave. If I could get somebody to go along with me, somebody to talk to, just so I wouldn't be all alone in there, I'd go; I'd crawl right in. A couple of times, it almost happened I did. The first time was back in 1938. The hurricane we had that fall damaged the roofs on a good many of the old South Street buildings, and the real-estate management company I rented this building from sent a man down here to see if my roof was all right. I asked the man why didn't he take the elevator up to the attic floor, there might be a door leading out on the roof. I told him I'd go along. He took one look inside the cage and said it would be more trouble than it was worth. What he did, he went up on the roof of the building next door and crossed over. Didn't find anything wrong. Six or seven months ago, I had another disappointment. I was talking with a customer of mine eats a fish lunch in here Fridays who's a contractor, and it happened I got on the subject of the upper floors, and he remarked he understood how I felt, my curiosity. He said he seldom passes an old boarded-up building without he wonders about it, wonders what it's like in there— all empty and hollow and dark and still, not a sound, only some rats maybe, racing around in the dark, or maybe some English sparrows flying around in there in the empty rooms that always get in if there's a crack in one of the boards over a broken window-pane, a crack or a knothole, and sometimes they can't find their way out and they keep on hopping and fly-ing and hopping and flying until they starve to death. He said he had been in many such buildings in the course of his work, and had seen some peculiar things. The next time he came in for lunch, he brought along a couple of those helmets that they wear around con-struction work, those orange-colored helmets, and he said to me, 'Come on, Louie. Put on one of these, and let's go up and try out that elevator. If the rope breaks, which I don't think it will—what the hell, a little shaking up is good for the liver. If the wheel drops, maybe these helmets will save us.' But he's a big heavy man, and he's not as active as he used to be. He went up the ladder first, and when he got to the top he backed right down. He put it on the basis he had a business appointment that afternoon and didn't want to get all dusty and dirty. I kept the helmets. He wanted them back, but I held on to them. I don't intend to let that elevator stand in my way much longer. One of these days, I'm going to sit down awhile with a bottle of Strega, and then I'm going to stick one of those helmets on my head and climb in that cage and put that damned elevator back in commission. The very least, I'll pull the rope and see what happens. I do wish I could find somebody had enough curiosity to go along with me. I've asked my waiters, and I've tried to interest some of the people in the market, but they all had the same answer. 'Hell, no,' they said."

Louie suddenly leaned forward. "What about you?" he asked. "Maybe I could persuade you."

I thought it over a few moments, and was about to suggest that we go upstairs at any rate and climb in the cage and look at the elevator, but just then a fishmonger who had finished his breakfast and wanted to pay his check rapped a dictatorial rat-a-tat on the glass top of the cigar showcase with a coin. Louie frowned and clenched his teeth. "I wish they wouldn't do that," he said, getting up. "It goes right through me."

. . .

Louie went over and took the man's money and gave him his change. Two waiters were standing at a service table in the rear, filling salt shakers, and Louie gestured to one of them to come up front and take charge of the cash register. Then he got himself another cup of coffee and sat back down and started talking again. "When I bought this restaurant," he said, "I wasn't too enthusiastic about the building. I had it in mind to build up the restaurant and find a location somewhere else in the market and move, the trade would follow. Instead of which, after a while I got very closely attached to the building. Why I did is one of those matters, it really doesn't make much sense. It's all mixed up with the name of a street in Brooklyn, and it goes back to the last place I worked in before I came here. That was Joe's in Brooklyn, the old Nevins Street Joe's, Nevins just off Flatbush Avenue Extension. I was a waiter there seven years, and it was the best place I ever worked in. Joe's is part of a chain now, the Brass Rail chain. In my time, it was run by a very high-type Italian restaurant man named Joe Sartori, and it was the biggest chophouse in Brooklyn—fifty waiters, a main floor, a balcony; a ladies' dining room, and a Roman Garden. Joe's was a hangout for Brooklyn political bosses and office-holders, and it got a class of trade we called the old Brooklyn family trade, the rich old intermarried families that made their money out of Brooklyn real estate and Brooklyn docks and Brooklyn streetcar lines and Brooklyn gasworks. They had their money sunk way down deep in Brooklyn. I don't know how it is now, they've probably all moved into apartment houses, but in those days a good many of them lived in steep-stoop, stain-glass mansions sitting up as solid as banks on Brooklyn Heights and Park Slope and over around Fort Greene Park. They were a big-eating class of people, and they believed in patronizing the good old Brooklyn restaurants. You'd see them in Joe's, and you'd seen them in Gage & Tollner's and Lundy's and Tappen's and Villepigue's. There was a high percentage of rich old independent women among them, widows and divorced ladies and maiden ladies. They were a class within a class. They wore clothes that hadn't been the style for years, and they wore the biggest hats I ever saw, and the ugliest. They all seemed to know each other since their childhood days, and they all had some peculiarity, and they all had one foot in the grave, and they all had big appetites. They had traveled widely, and they were good judges of food, and they knew how to order a meal. Some were poison, to say the least, and some were just as nice as they could be. On the whole, I liked them; they broke the monotony. Some always came to my station; if my tables were full, they'd sit in some leather chairs Mr. Sartori had up front and wait. One was a widow named Mrs. Frelinghuysen. She was very old and tiny and delicate, and she ate like a horse. She ate like she thought any meal might be her last meal. She was a little lame from rheumatism, and she used a walking stick that had a snake's head for a knob, a snake's head carved out of ivory. She had a pleasant voice, a beautiful voice, and she made the most surprising funny remarks. They were coarse remarks, the humor in them. She made some remarks on occasion that had me wondering did I hear right. Everybody liked her, the way she hung on to life; and everybody tried to do things for her. I remember Mr. Sartori one night went out in the rain and got her a cab. 'She's such a thin little thing,' he said when he came back in. 'There's nothing to her,' he said, 'but six bones and one gut and a set of teeth and a big hat with a bird on it.' Her peculiarity was she always brought her own silver. It was old family silver. She'd have it wrapped up in a linen napkin in her handbag, and she'd get it out and set her own place. After she finished eating, I'd take it to the kitchen and wash it, and she'd stuff it back in her handbag. She'd always start off with one dozen oysters in winter or one dozen clams in summer, and she'd gobble them down and go on from there. She could get more out of a lobster than anybody I ever saw. You'd think she'd got everything she possibly could, and then she'd pull the little legs off that most people don't even bother with, and suck the juice out of them. Sometimes, if it was a slow night and I was just standing around, she'd call me over and talk to me while she ate. She'd talk about people and past times, and she knew a lot; she had kept her eyes open while she was going through life.

"My hours in Joe's were ten in the morning to nine at night. In the afternoons, I'd take a break from three to four-thirty. I saw so much rich food I usually didn't want any lunch, the way old waiters get—just a crust of bread, or some fruit. If it was a nice day, I'd step over to Albee Square and go into an old fancy-fruit store named Ecklebe & Guyer's and pick me out a piece of fruit—an orange or two, or a bunch of grapes, or one of those big red pomegranates that split open when they're ripe the same as figs and their juice is so strong and red it purifies the blood. Then I'd go over to Schermerhorn Street. Schermerhorn was a block and a half west of Joe's. There were some trees along Schermerhorn, and some benches under the trees. Young women would sit along there with their babies, and old men would sit along there the whole day through and read papers and play checkers and discuss matters. And I'd sit there the little time I had and rest my feet and eat my fruit and read the *New York Times*—my purpose reading the *New York Times,* I was trying to improve my English. Schermerhorn Street was a peaceful old backwater street, so nice and quiet, and I liked it. It did me good to sit down there and rest. One afternoon the thought occurred to me, 'Who the hell was Schermerhorn?' So that night it happened Mrs. Frelinghuysen was in, and I asked her who was Schermerhorn that the street's named for. She knew, all right. Oh, Jesus, she more than knew. She saw I was interested, and from then on that was one of the main subjects she talked to me about—Old New York street names and neighborhood names; Old New York this, Old New York that. She knew a great many facts and figures and skeletons in the closet that her mother and her grandmother and her aunts had passed on down to her relating to the old New York Dutch families that they call the Knickerbockers—those that dissipated too much and dissipated all their property away and died out and disappeared, and those that are still around. Holland Dutch, not German Dutch, the way I used to think it meant. The Schermerhorns are one of the oldest of the old Dutch families, according to her, and one of the best. They were big landowners in Dutch days, and they still are, and they go back so deep in Old New York that if you went any deeper you wouldn't find anything but Indians and bones and bears. Mrs. Frelinghuysen was well acquainted with the Schermerhorn family. She had been to Schermerhorn weddings and Schermerhorn funerals. I remember she told about a Schermerhorn girl she went to school with who belonged to the eighth generation, I think it was, in direct descent from old Jacob Schermerhorn who came here from Schermerhorn, Holland, in the sixteen-thirties, and this girl died and was buried in the Schermerhorn plot in Trinity Church cemetery up in Washington Heights, and one day many years later driving down from Connecticut Mrs. Frelinghuysen got to thinking about her and stopped off at the cemetery and looked around in there and located her grave and put some jonquils on it."

At this moment a fishmonger opened the door of the restaurant and put his head in and interrupted Louie. "Hey, Louie," he called out, "has Little Joe been in?"

"Little Joe that's a lumper on the pier," asked Louie, "or Little Joe that works for Chesebro, Robbins?"

"The lumper," said the fishmonger.

"He was in and out an hour ago," said Louie. "He snook in and got a cup of coffee and was out and gone the moment he finished it."

"If you see him," the fishmonger said, "tell him they want him on the pier. A couple of draggers just came in—the *Felicia* from New Bedford and the *Positive* from Gloucester—and the *Ann Elizabeth Kristin* from Stonington is out in the river, on her way in."

Louie nodded, and the fishmonger went away. "To continue about Mrs. Frelinghuysen," Louie said, "she died in 1927. The next year, I got married. The next year was the year the stock market crashed. The next year, I quit Joe's and came over here and bought this restaurant and rented this building. I rented it from a real-estate company, the Charles F. Noyes Company, and I paid my rent to them, and I took it for granted they owned it. One afternoon four years later, the early part of 1934, around in March, I was standing at the cash register in here and a long black limousine drove up out front and parked, and a uniform chauffeur got out and came in and said Mrs. Schermerhorn wanted to speak to me, and I looked at him and said, 'What do you mean—Mrs. Schermerhorn?' And he said, 'Mrs. Schermerhorn that owns this building.' So I went out on the sidewalk, and there was a lady sitting in the limousine, her appearance was quite beautiful, and she said she was Mrs. Arthur F. Schermerhorn and her husband had died in September the year before and she was taking a look at some of the buildings the estate owned and the Noyes company was the agent for. So she asked me some questions concerning what shape the building was in, and the like of that. Which I answered to the best of my ability. Then I told her I was certainly surprised for various reasons to hear this was Schermerhorn property. I told her, 'Frankly,' I said, 'I'm amazed to hear it.' I asked her did she know anything about the history of the building, how old it was, and she said she didn't, she hadn't ever even seen it before, it was just one of a number of properties that had come down to her husband from his father. Even her husband, she said, she doubted if he had known much about the building. I had a lot of questions I wanted to ask, and I asked her to get out and come in and have some coffee and take a look around, but I guess she figured the signboard SLOPPY LOUIE'S RESTAURANT meant what it said. She thanked me and said she had to be getting on, and she gave the chauffeur an address, and they drove off and I never saw her again.

"I went back inside and stood there and thought it over, and the effect it had on me, the simple fact my building was an old Schermerhorn building, it may sound foolish, but it pleased me very much. The feeling I had, it connected me with the past. It connected me with Old New York. It connected Sloppy Louie's Restaurant with Old New York. It made the building look much better to me. Instead of just an old run-down building in the fish market, the way it looked to me before, it had a history to it, connections going back, and I liked that. It stirred up my curiosity to know more. A day or so later, I went over and asked the people at the Noyes company would they mind telling me something about the history of the building, but they didn't know anything about it. They had only took over the management of it in 1929, the year before I rented it, and the company that had been the previous agent had gone out of business. They said to go to the City Department of Buildings in the Municipal Building. Which I did, but the man in there, he looked up my building and couldn't find any file on it, and he said it's hard to date a good many old buildings down in my part of town because a fire in the Building Department around 1890 destroyed some cases of papers relating to them—permits and specifications and all that. He advised me to go to the Hall of Records on Chambers Street, where deeds are recorded. I went over there, and they showed me the deed, but it wasn't any help. It described the lot, but all it said about the building, it said 'the building thereon,' and didn't give any date on it. So I gave up. Well, there's a nice old gentleman eats in here sometimes who works for the Title Guarantee & Trust Company, an old Yankee fish-eater, and we were talking one day, and it happened he told me that Title Guarantee has tons and tons of records on New York City property stored away in their vaults that they refer to when they're deciding whether or not the title to a piece of property is clear. 'Do me a favor,' I said, 'and look up the records on 92 South Street—nothing private or financial; just the history—and I'll treat you to the best broiled lobster you ever had. I'll treat you to broiled lobster six Fridays in a row,' I said, 'and I'll broil the lobsters myself.'

"The next time he came in, he said he had took a look in the Title Guarantee vaults for me, and had talked to a title searcher over there who's an expert on South Street property, and he read me off some notes he had made. It seems all this end of South Street used to be under water. The East River flowed over it. Then the city filled it in and divided it into lots. In February, 1804, a merchant by the name of Peter Schermerhorn, a descendant of Jacob Schermerhorn, was given grants to the lot my building now stands on—92 South—and the lot next to it—93 South, a corner lot, the corner of South and Fulton. Schermerhorn put up a four-story brick-and-frame building on each of these lots—stores on the street floors and flats above. In 1872, 1873, or 1874—my friend from Title Guarantee wasn't able to determine the exact year—the heirs and assigns of Peter Schermerhorn ripped these buildings down and put up two six-story brick buildings exactly alike side by side on 92 and 93. Those buildings are this one here and the one next door. The Schermerhorns put them up for hotel purposes, and they were designed so they could be used as one building— there's a party wall between them, and in those days there were sets of doors on each floor leading from one building to the other. This building had that old hand-pull elevator in it from bottom to top, and the other building had a wide staircase in it from bottom to top. The Schermerhorns didn't skimp on materials; they used heart pine for beams and they used hand-molded, air-dried, kiln-burned Hudson River brick. The Schermerhorns leased the buildings to two hotel men named Frederick and Henry Lemmermann, and the first lease on record is 1874. The name of the hotel was the Fulton Ferry Hotel. The hotel saloon occupied the whole bottom floor of the building next door, and the hotel restaurant was right in here, and they had a combined lobby and billiard room that occupied the second floor of both buildings, and they had a reading room in the front half of the third floor of this building and rooms in the rear half, and all the rest of the space in both buildings was single rooms and double rooms and suites. At that time, there were passenger-line steamship docks all along South Street, lines that went to every part of the world, and out-of-town people waiting for passage on the various steamers would stay at the Fulton Ferry Hotel. Also, the Brooklyn Bridge hadn't yet been built, and the Fulton Ferry was the principal ferry to Brooklyn, and the ferryhouse stood directly in front of the hotel. On account of the ferry, Fulton Street was like a funnel; damned near everything headed for Brooklyn went through it. It was full of foot traffic and horse-drawn traffic day and night, and South and Fulton was one of the most ideal saloon corners in the city.

"The Fulton Ferry Hotel lasted forty-five years, but it only had about twenty good years; the rest was downhill. The first bad blow was the bridges over the East River, beginning with the Brooklyn Bridge, that gradually drained off the heavy traffic on the Fulton Ferry that the hotel saloon got most of its trade from. And then, the worst blow of all, the passenger lines began leaving South Street and moving around to bigger, longer docks on the Hudson. Little by little, the Fulton Ferry Hotel got to be one of those waterfront hotels that rummies hole up in, and old men on pensions, and old nuts, and sailors on the beach. Steps going down. Around 1910, somewhere in there, the Lemmermanns gave up the part of the hotel that was in this building, and the Schermerhorn interests boarded up the windows on the four upper floors and bricked up the doors in the party wall connecting the two buildings. And the hotel restaurant, what they did with that, they rented it to a man named MacDonald who turned it into a quick lunch for the people in the fish market. MacDonald ran it awhile. Then a son of his took it over, according to some lease notations in the Title Guarantee records. Then a man named Jimmy Something-or-Other took it over. It was called Jimmy's while he had it. Then two Greek fellows took it over. Then a German fellow and his wife and sister and brother-in-law had it awhile. Then two brothers named Fortunato and Louie Barbagelata took it over. Then John Barbagelata took it over, a nephew of the other Barbagelatas, and eventually I came along and bought the lease and furnishings off of him. After the party wall was bricked up, the Lemmermanns held on to the building next door a few years more, and kept on calling it the Fulton Ferry Hotel, but all it amounted to, it was just a waterfront saloon with rooms for rent up above. They operated it until 1919, when the final blow hit them—prohibition. Those are the bare bones of the matter. If I could get upstairs just once in that damned old elevator and scratch around in those hotel registers up there and whatever to hell else is stored up there, it might be possible I'd find out a whole lot more."

"Look, Louie," I said, "I'll go up in the elevator with you."

"You think you would," Louie said, "but you'd just take a look at it, and then you'd back out."

"I'd like to see inside the cage, at least," I said.

Louie looked at me inquisitively. "You really want to go up there?" he asked.

"Yes," I said.

"The next time you come down here, put on the oldest clothes you got, so the dust don't make any difference," Louie said, "and we'll go up and try out the elevator."

"Oh, no," I said. "Now or never. If I think it over, I'll change my mind."

"It's your own risk," he said.

"Of course," I said.

Louie abruptly stood up. "Let me speak to the waiter at the cash register," he said, "and I'll be with you."

He went over and spoke to the waiter. Then he opened the door of a cupboard in back of the cash register and took out two flashlights and the two construction-work helmets that his customer, the contractor, had brought in. He handed me one of the flashlights and one of the helmets. I put the helmet on and started over to a mirror to see how I looked. "Come on," Louie said, somewhat impatiently. We went up the stairs to the second floor. Along one wall, on this floor, were shelves stacked with restaurant supplies—canned goods and nests of bowls and plates and boxes of soap powder and boxes of paper napkins. Headed up against the wainscoting were half a dozen burlap bags of potatoes. A narrow, round-runged, wooden ladder stood at a slant in a corner up front, and Louie went directly to it. One end of the ladder was fixed to the floor, and the other end was fixed to the ceiling. At the top of the ladder, flush with the ceiling, was the bottom of the elevator cage with the trap door cut in it. The trap door was shut. Louie unbuttoned a shirt button and stuck his flashlight in the front of his shirt, and immediately started up the ladder. At the top, he paused and looked down at me for an instant. His face was set. Then he gave the trap door a shove, and it fell back, and a cloud of black dust burst out. Louie ducked his head and shook it and blew the dust out of his nose. He stood at the top of the ladder for about a minute, waiting for the dust to settle. Then, all of a sudden, he scrambled into the cage. "Oh, God in Heaven," he called out, "the dust in here! It's like somebody emptied a vacuum-cleaner bag in here." I climbed the ladder and entered the cage and closed the trap door. Louie pointed his flashlight up the shaft. "I thought there was only one wheel up there," he said, peering upward. "I see two." The dust had risen to the top of the shaft, and we couldn't see the wheels clearly. There was an iron strut over the top of the cage, and a cable extended from it to one of the wheels. Two thick hemp ropes hung down into the cage from the other wheel. "I'm going to risk it," Louie said. "I'm going to pull the rope. Take both flashlights, and shine one on me and shine the other up the shaft. If I can get the cage up about a foot, it'll be level with the third floor, and we can open the door."

Louie grasped one of the ropes and pulled on it, and dust sprang off it all the way to the top. The wheel screeched as the rope turned it, but the cage didn't move. "The rope feels loose," Louie said. "I don't think it has any grip on the wheel." He pulled again, and nothing happened.

"Maybe you've got the wrong rope," I said.

He disregarded me and pulled again, and the cage shook from side to side. Louie let go of the rope, and looked up the shaft. "That wheel acts all right," he said. He pulled the rope again, and this time the cage rose an inch or two. He pulled five or six times, and the cage rose an inch or two each time. Then we looked down and saw that the floor of the cage was almost even with the third floor. Louie pulled the rope once more. Then he stepped over and pushed on the grilled door of the cage and shook it, trying to swing it open; it rattled, and long, lacy flakes of rust fell off it, but it wouldn't open. I gave Louie the lights of both flashlights, and he examined the door. There were sets of hinges down it in two places. "I see," Louie said. "You're supposed to fold it back in." The hinges were stiff, and he got in a frenzy struggling with the door before he succeeded in folding it back far enough for us to get through. On the landing there was a kind of storm-door-like affair, a three-sided cubbyhole with a plain wooden door in the center side. "I guess they had that there to keep people from falling in the shaft," Louie said. "It'll be just our luck the door's locked on the other side. If it is, I'm not going to monkey around; I'm going to kick it in." He tried the knob, and it turned, and he opened the door, and we walked out and entered the front half of the third floor, the old reading room of the Fulton Ferry Hotel.

It was pitch-dark in the room. We stood still and played the lights of our flashlights across the floor and up and down the walls. Everything we saw was covered with dust. There was a thick, black mat of fleecy dust on the floor—dust and soot and grit and lint and slut's wool. Louie scuffed his shoes in it. "A-a-ah!" he said, and spat. His light fell on a roll-top desk, and he hurried over to it and rolled the top up. I stayed where I was, and continued to look around. The room was rectangular, and it had a stamped-tin ceiling, and tongue-and-groove wainscoting, and plaster walls the color of putty. The plaster had crumbled down to the laths in many places. There was a gas fixture on each wall. High up on one wall was a round hole that had once held a stove-pipe. Screwed to the door leading to the rear half of the floor were two framed signs. One said, "THIS READING ROOM WILL BE CLOSED AT 1 A.M. FULTON FERRY HOTEL." The other said, "ALL GAMBLING IN THIS READING ROOM STRICTLY PROHIBITED. BY ORDER OF THE PROPRIETORS. FULTON FERRY HOTEL. F. & H. LEMMERMANN, PROPRIETORS." Some bedsprings and some ugly white knobby iron bedsteads were stacked criss-cross in one corner. The stack was breast-high. Between the boarded-up windows, against the front wall, stood a marble-top table. On it were three seltzer bottles with corroded spouts, a tin water cooler painted to resemble brown marble, a cracked glass bell of the kind used to cover clocks and stuffed birds, and four sugar bowls whose metal flap lids had been eaten away from their hinges by rust. On the floor, beside the table, were an umbrella stand, two brass spittoons, and a wire basket filled to the brim with whiskey bottles of the flask type. I took the bottles out one by one. Dampness had destroyed the labels; pulpy scraps of paper with nothing legible on them were sticking to a few on the bottom. Lined up back to back in the middle of the room were six bureaus with mirrors on their tops. Still curious to see how I looked in the construction-work helmet, I went and peered in one of the mirrors.

Louie, who had been yanking drawers out of the roll-top desk, suddenly said, "God damn it! I thought I'd find those hotel registers in here. There's nothing in here, only rusty paper clips." He went over to the whiskey bottles I had strewn about and examined a few, and then he walked up behind me and looked in the mirror. His face was strained. He had rubbed one cheek with his dusty fingers, and it was streaked with dust. "We're the first faces to look in that mirror in years and years," he said. He held his flashlight with one hand and jerked open the top drawer of the bureau with the other. There were a few hairpins in the drawer, and some buttons, and a comb with several teeth missing, and a needle with a bit of black thread in its eye, and a scattering of worn playing cards; the design on the backs of the cards was a stag at bay. He opened the middle drawer, and it was empty. He opened the bottom drawer, and it was empty. He started in on the next bureau. In the top drawer, he found a square, clear-glass medicine bottle that contained two inches of colorless liquid and half an inch of black sediment. He wrenched the stopper out, and put the bottle to his nose and smelled the liquid. "It's gone dead," he said. "It doesn't smell like anything at all." He poured the liquid on the floor, and handed the bottle to me. Blown in one side of it was "Perry's Pharmacy. Open All Night. Popular Prices. World Building, New York." All at once, while looking at the old bottle, I became conscious of the noises of the market seemingly far below, and I stepped over to one of the boarded-up windows and tried to peep down at South Street through a split in a board, but it wasn't possible. Louie continued to go through the bureau drawers. "Here's something," he said. "Look at this." He handed me a foxed and yellowed photograph of a dark young woman with upswept hair who wore a lace shirtwaist and a long black skirt and sat in a fanciful fan-backed wicker chair. After a while, Louie reached the last drawer in the last bureau, and looked in it and snorted and slammed it shut. "Let's go in the rear part of the floor," he said.

Louie opened the door, and we entered a hall, along which was a row of single rooms. There were six rooms, and on their doors were little oval enameled number plates running from 12 to 17. We looked in Room 12. Two wooden coat hangers were lying on the floor. Room 13 was absolutely empty. Room 14 had evidently last been occupied by someone with a religious turn of mind. There was an old iron bedstead still standing in it, but without springs, and tacked on the wall above the head of the bed was a placard of the kind distributed by some evangelistic religious groups. It said, "The Wages of Sin is Death; but the Gift of God is Eternal Life through Jesus Christ our Lord." Tacked on the wall beside the bed was another religious placard: "Christ is the Head of this House, the Unseen Host at Every Meal, the Silent Listener to Every Conversation." We stared at the placards a few moments, and then Louie turned and started back up the hall.

"Louie," I called, following him, "where are you going?"

"Let's go on back downstairs," he said.

"I thought we were going on up to the floors

above," I said. "Let's go up to the fourth floor, at least. We'll take turns pulling the rope."

"There's nothing up here," he said. "I don't want to stay up here another minute. Come on, let's go."

I followed him into the elevator cage. "I'll pull the rope going down," I said.

Louie said nothing, and I glanced at him. He was leaning against the side of the cage, and his shoulders were slumped and his eyes were tired. "I didn't learn much I didn't know before," he said.

"You learned that the wages of sin is death," I said, trying to say something cheerful.

"I knew that before," Louie said. A look of revulsion came on his face. "The wages of sin!" he said. "Sin, death, dust, old empty rooms, old empty whiskey bottles, old empty bureau drawers. Come on, pull the rope faster! Pull it faster! Let's get out of this."

(1952)

The Bottom of
the Harbor

The bulk of the water in New York Harbor is oily, dirty, and germy. Men on the mud suckers, the big harbor dredges, like to say that you could bottle it and sell it for poison. The bottom of the harbor is dirtier than the water. In most places, it is covered with a blanket of sludge that is composed of silt, sewage, industrial wastes, and clotted oil. The sludge is thickest in the slips along the Hudson, in the flats on the Jersey side of the Upper Bay, and in backwaters such as Newtown Creek, Wallabout Bay, and the Gowanus Canal. In such areas, where it isn't exposed to the full sweep of the tides, it accumulates rapidly. In Wallabout Bay, a nook in the East River that is part of the Brooklyn Navy Yard, it accumulates at the rate of a foot and half a year. The sludge rots in warm weather and from it gas-filled bubbles as big as basketballs continually surge to the surface. Dredgemen call them "sludge bubbles." Occasionally, a bubble upsurges so furiously that it brings a mass of sludge along with it. In midsummer, here and there in the harbor, the rising and breaking of sludge bubbles makes the water seethe and spit. People sometimes stand on the coal and lumber quays that line the Gowanus Canal and stare at the black, bubbly water.

Nevertheless, there is considerable marine life in the harbor water and on the harbor bottom. Under the paths of liners and tankers and ferries and tugs, fish school and oysters spawn and lobsters nest. There are clams on the sludgy bottom, and mussels and mud shrimp and conchs and crabs and sea worms and sea plants. Bedloe's Island, the Statue of Liberty island, is in a part of the harbor that is grossly polluted, but there is a sprinkling of soft-shell clams in the mud beneath the shallow water that surrounds it. The ebb of a spring tide always draws the water off a broad strip of this mud, and then flocks of gulls appear from all over the Upper Bay and light on it and thrash around and scratch for clams. They fly up with clams in their beaks and drop them on the concrete walk that runs along the top of the island's sea wall, and then they swoop down and pluck the meats out of the broken shells. Even in the Gowanus Canal, there are a few fish; the water is dead up at the head of it—only germs can live there—but from the crook at the Sixth Street Basin on down to the mouth there are cunners and tomcods and eels. The cunners nibble on the acorn barnacles on the piles under the old quays.

In the spring, summer, and fall, during the great coastwise and inshore and offshore migrations of fishes along the Middle Atlantic Coast, at least three dozen species enter the harbor. Only a few members of some species show up. Every spring, a few long, jaggy-backed sea sturgeon show up. Every summer, in the Lower Bay, dragger nets bring up a few small, weird, brightly colored strays from Southern waters, such as porcupine fish, scorpion fish, triggerfish, lookdowns, halfbeaks, hairtails, and goggle-eyed scad. Every fall, a few tuna show up. Other species show up in the hundreds of thousands or in the millions. Among these are shad, cod, whiting, porgy, blackback flounder, summer herring, alewife, sea bass, ling, mackerel, butterfish, and blackfish. Some years, one species, the mossbunker, shows up in the hundreds of millions. The mossbunker is a kind of herring that weighs around a pound when full-grown. It migrates in enormous schools and is caught in greater quantity than any other fish on the Atlantic Coast, but it is unfamiliar to the general public because it isn't a good table fish; it is too oily and bony. It is a factory fish; it is converted into an oil that is used in making soaps, paints, and printing inks (which is why some newspapers have a fishy smell on damp days), and into a meal that is fed to pigs and poultry. In the summer and fall, scores of schools of mossbunkers are hemmed in and caught in the Lower Bay, Sandy Hook Bay, and Raritan Bay by fleets of purse seiners with Negro crews that work out of little fishing ports in North Carolina, Virginia, Delaware, New Jersey, and Long Island and rove up and down the coast, following the schools.

The migratory fishes enter the harbor to spawn or to feed. Some mill around in the bays and river mouths for a few days and leave; some stay for months. Only one fish, the eel, is present in great numbers in all seasons. Eels are nocturnal scavengers, and they thrive in the harbor. They live on the bottom, and it makes no difference to them how deep or dirty it is. They live in ninety feet of water in the cable area of the Narrows and they live in a foot of water in tide ditches in the Staten Island marshes; they live in clean blue water in Sandy Hook Bay and they live around the outfalls of sewers in the East River. There are eight or nine hundred old hulks in the harbor. A few are out in the bays, deeply submerged, but most of them lie half sunk behind the pierhead line in the Jersey Flats and the flats along the Arthur Kill and the Kill van Kull—old scows and barges, old boxcar floats, old tugs, old ferryboats, old sidewheel excursion steamers, old sailing ships. They were towed into the flats and left to rot. They are full of holes; the water in the hulls of many of them rises and falls with the tides. Some are choked with sea lettuce and sea slime. In the summer, multitudes of eels lay up in the hulks during the day and wriggle out at night to feed. In the winter, they bed down in the hulks and hibernate. When they begin to hibernate, usually around the middle of December, they are at their best; they are fleshy then, and tender and sweet. At that time, Italian-Americans and German-Americans from every part of Staten Island go to certain old scows in the flats along the kills and spear so many eels that they bring them home in washtubs and potato sacks. The harbor eels—that is, the eels that live in the harbor the year round—are all males, or bucks. The females, or roes, until they become mature, live in rivers and creeks and ponds, up in fresh water. They become mature after they have spent from seven to thirteen years in fresh water. Every fall, thousands upon thousands of mature females run down the rivers that empty into the harbor—the Hudson, the Hackensack, the Passaic, the Elizabeth, the Rahway, and the Raritan. When they reach salt water, they lie still awhile and rest. They may rest for a few hours or a few days. Divers say that some days in October and November it is impossible to move about anywhere on the harbor bottom without stirring up throngs of big, fat, silver-bellied female eels. After resting, the females congregate with the mature harbor males, and they go out to sea together to spawn.

Hard-shell clams, or quahogs, the kind that appear on menus as littlenecks and cherrystones, are extraordinarily abundant in the harbor. Sanitary engineers classify the water in a number of stretches of the Lower Bay and Jamaica Bay as "moderately polluted." In these stretches, on thinly sludge-coated bottoms, under water that ranges in depth from one to thirty-five feet, are several vast, pullulating, mazy networks of hard-shell-clam beds. On some beds, the clams are crowded as tightly together as cobblestones. They are lovely clams—the inner lips of their shells have a lustrous violet border, and their meats are as pink and plump as rosebuds—but they are unsafe; they sometimes contain the germs of a variety of human diseases, among them bacillary and protozoal dysentery and typhoid fever, that they collect in their systems while straining nourishment out of the dirty water. The polluted beds have been condemned for over thirty years, and are guarded against poachers by the city Department of Health and the state Conservation Department. Quite a few people in waterfront neighborhoods in Staten Island, Brooklyn, and Queens have never been fully convinced that the clams are unsafe. On moonless nights and foggy days, they slip out, usually in rowboats, and raid the beds. In the course of a year, they take tons of clams. They eat them in chowders and stews, and they eat them raw. Every once in a while, whole families get horribly sick.

Just west of the mouth of the harbor, between Sandy Hook and the south shore of Staten Island, there is an area so out-of-the-way that anchorage grounds have long been set aside in it for ships and barges loaded with dynamite and other explosives. In this area, there are three small tracts of clean, sparkling, steel-blue water, about fifteen square miles in all. This is the only unpolluted water in the harbor. One tract of about five square miles, in Raritan Bay, belongs to the State of New York; the others, partly in Raritan Bay and partly in Sandy Hook Bay, belong to New Jersey. The bottoms of these tracts are free of sludge, and there are some uncontaminated hard-shell-clam beds on them. They are public beds; after taking out a license, residents of the state in whose waters they lie may harvest and sell clams from them. The New York beds are clammed by about a hundred and fifty Staten Islanders, most of whom live in or near the sleepy little south-shore ports of Prince's Bay and Great Kills. Some do seasonal work in shipyards, on fishing boats, or on truck farms, and clam in slack times, and some—thirty or so, mostly older men—clam steadily. They go out at dawn in sea skiffs and in rowboats equipped with outboard motors. When they reach the beds, they scatter widely and anchor. They lean over the sides of their boats and rake the bottom with clumsy rakes, called Shinnecock rakes, that have twenty-four-foot handles and long, inturned teeth. Last year, they raked up eighteen thousand bushels. A soup factory in New Jersey bought about half of these, and the rest went to fish stores and hotels and restaurants, mainly in New York City. Every New Yorker who frequently eats clams on the half shell has most likely eaten at least a few that came out of the harbor.

In Dutch and English days, immense beds of oysters grew in the harbor. They bordered the shores of Brooklyn and Queens, and they encircled Manhattan, Staten Island, and the islands in the Upper Bay; to the Dutch, Ellis Island was Oyster Island and Bedloe's Island was Great Oyster Island. One chain of beds extended from Sandy Hook straight across the harbor and up the Hudson to Ossining. The Dutch and the English were, as they still are, gluttonous oyster eaters. By the end of the eighteenth century, all but the deepest of the beds had been stripped. Oysters, until then among the cheapest of foods, gradually became expensive. In the eighteen-twenties, a group of Staten Island shipowners began to buy immature oysters by the schooner-load in other localities and

bring them to New York and bed them in the harbor
until they got their growth, when they were tonged
up and shipped to the wholesale oyster market in
Manhattan, to cities in the Middle West, and to
London, where they were prized. This business was
known as bedding. The bedders obtained most of
their seed stock in Chesapeake Bay and in several
New Jersey and Long Island bays. Some bought
three-year-olds and put them down for only six or
seven months, and some bought younger oysters and
put them down for longer periods. At first, the bedders used the shoals in the Kill van Kull, but by and
by they found that the best bottoms lay along the sea-
ward side of Staten Island, in the Lower Bay and
Raritan Bay. Back then, the inshore water in these
bays was rich in diatoms and protozoa, the tiny plants
and animals on which oysters feed. Spread out in this
water, on clean bottoms, at depths averaging around
thirteen feet, oysters matured and fattened much
faster than they did crowded together on their shell-
cluttered spawning grounds; a thousand bushels of
three-year-olds from Chesapeake Bay, put down in
April in a favorable season, might amount to fourteen
hundred bushels when taken up in October. Bedding
was highly profitable in good years and many for-
tunes were made in it. It was dominated by old-
settler Staten Island families—the Tottens, the
Winants, the De Harts, the Deckers, the Manees, the

Mersereaus, the Van Wyks, the Van Duzers, the Latourettes, the Housmans, the Bedells, and the Depews. It lasted for almost a century, during which, at one time or another, five Staten Island ports—Mariner's Harbor, Port Richmond, Great Kills, Prince's Bay, and Tottenville—had oyster docks and fleets of schooners, sloops, and tonging skiffs. Prince's Bay had the biggest fleet and the longest period of prosperity; on menus in New York and London, harbor oysters were often called Prince's Bays. Approximately nine thousand acres of harbor bottom, split up into plots varying from a fraction of an acre to four hundred acres, were used for beds. The plots were leased from the state and were staked with a forest of hemlock poles; nowadays, in deepening and widening Ambrose Channel, Chapel Hill Channel, Swash Channel, and other ship channels in the Lower Bay, dredges occasionally dig up the tubeworm-incrusted stumps of old boundary poles. Bedding was most prosperous in the thirty years between 1860 and 1890. In good years in that period, as many as fifteen hundred men were employed on the beds and as many as five hundred thousand bushels of oysters were marketed. Some years, as much as a third of the crop was shipped to Billingsgate, the London fish market. For a while, the principal bedders were the richest men on Staten Island. They put their money in waterfront real estate, they named streets after themselves, and they built big, showy wooden mansions. A half dozen of these mansions still stand in a blighted neighborhood in Mariner's Harbor, in among refineries and coal tipples and junk yards. One has a widow's walk, two have tall fluted columns, all have oddly shaped gables, and all are decorated with scroll-saw work. They overlook one of the oiliest and gummiest stretches of the Kill van Kull. On the south shore, in the sassafras barrens west of Prince's Bay, there are three more of these mansions, all empty. Their fanlights are broken, their shutters swag, and their yards are a tangle of weeds and vines and overturned birdbaths and dead pear trees.

After 1900, as more and more of the harbor became polluted, people began to grow suspicious of harbor oysters, and the bedding business declined. In the summer of 1916, a number of cases of typhoid fever were traced beyond all doubt to the eating of oysters that had been bedded on West Bank Shoal, in the Lower Bay, and it was found that sewage from a huge New Jersey trunk sewer whose outfall is at the confluence of the Kill van Kull and the Upper Bay was being swept through the Narrows and over the beds by the tides. The Department of Health thereupon condemned the beds and banned the business. The bedders were allowed to take up the oysters they had down and rebed them in clean water in various

Long Island bays. They didn't get them all, of course. A few were missed and left behind on every bed. Some of these propagated, and now their descendants are sprinkled over shoaly areas in all the bays below the Narrows. They are found on West Bank Shoal, East Bank Shoal, Old Orchard Shoal, Round Shoal, Flynns Knoll, and Romer Shoal. They live in clumps and patches; a clump may have several dozen oysters in it and a patch may have several hundred. Divers and dredgemen call them wild oysters. It is against state and city laws to "dig, rake, tong, or otherwise remove" these oysters from the water. A few elderly men who once were bedders are still living in the old Staten Island oyster ports, and many sons and grandsons of bedders. They have a proprietary feeling about harbor oysters, and every so often, in cold weather, despite the laws, some of them go out to the old, ruined beds and poach a mess. They know what they are doing; they watch the temperature of the water to make sure the oysters are "sleeping," or hibernating, before they eat any. Oysters shut their shells and quit feeding and begin to hibernate when the temperature of the water in which they lie goes down to forty-one degrees; in three or four days, they free themselves of whatever germs they may have taken in, and then they are clean and safe.

There is a physician in his late fifties in St. George

whose father and grandfather were bedders. On a wall of his waiting room hangs an heirloom, a chart of oyster plots on West Bank Shoal that was made in 1886 by a marine surveyor for the state; it is wrinkled and finger-smudged and salt-water-spotted, and his grandfather's plot, which later became his father's—a hundred and two acres on the outer rim of the shoal, down below Swinburne Island—is bounded on it in red ink. The physician keeps a sea skiff in one of the south-shore ports and goes fishing every decent Sunday. He stores a pair of pole-handled tongs in the skiff and sometimes spends a couple of hours hunting for clumps of harbor oysters. One foggy Sunday afternoon last March, he got in his skiff, with a companion, and remarked to the people on the dock that he was going codfishing on the Scallop Ridge, off Rockaway Beach. Instead, picking his way through the fog, he went up to the West Bank and dropped anchor on one of his father's old beds and began tonging. He made over two dozen grabs and moved the skiff four times before he located a clump. It was a big clump, and he tonged up all the oysters in it; there were exactly sixty. All were mature, all were speckled with little holes made by boring sponges, and all were wedge-shaped. Sea hair, a marine weed, grew thickly on their shells. One was much bigger than the others, and the physician picked it up and smoothed aside its mat of coarse, black, curly sea hair and counted the ridges on its upper shell and said that it was at least fourteen years old. "It's too big to eat on the half shell," he told his companion. He bent over the gunnel of the skiff and gently put it back in the water. Then he selected a dozen that ranged in age from four to seven years and opened them. Their meats were well developed and gray-green and glossy. He ate one with relish. "Every time I eat harbor oysters," he said, "my childhood comes floating up from the bottom of my mind." He reflected for a few moments. "They have a high iodine content," he continued, "and they have a characteristic taste. When I was a boy in Prince's Bay, the old bedders used to say that they tasted like almonds. Since the water went bad, that taste has become more pronounced. It's become coppery and bitter. If you've ever tasted the little nut that's inside the pit of a peach, the kernel, that's how they taste."

The fish and shellfish in the harbor and in the ocean just outside provide all or part of a living for about fifteen hundred men who call themselves baymen. They work out of bays and inlets and inlets within inlets along the coasts of Staten Island, Brooklyn, and Queens. Some baymen clam on the public beds. Some baymen set eelpots. Some baymen set pound nets, or fish traps. Pound nets are strung from labyrinths of stakes in shoal areas, out of the way of the harbor traffic. Last year, during the shad, summer herring, and mossbunker migrations, forty-one of them were set off the Staten Island coast, between Midland Beach and Great Kills, in an old oyster-bedding area. Some baymen go out in draggers, or small trawlers, of which there are two fleets in the harbor. One fleet has sixteen boats, and ties up at two shaky piers on Plumb Beach Channel, an inlet just east of Sheepshead Bay, on the Brooklyn coast. The other has nine boats, and ties up alongside a quay on the west branch of Mill Basin, a three-branched inlet in the bulrush marshes in the Flatlands neighbor-hood of Brooklyn. The majority of the men in both fleets are Italian-Americans, a few of whom in their youth fished out of the Sicilian ports of Palermo and Castellammare del Golfo. Some of them tack saints' pictures and miraculous medals and scapular medals and little evil-eye amulets on the walls of their pilot-houses. The amulets are in the shape of hunchbacks, goat horns, fists with two fingers upraised, and opened scissors; they come from stores on Mulberry Street and are made of plastic. The harbor draggers range from thirty to fifty feet and carry two to five men. According to the weather and the season, they drag their baglike nets in the Lower Bay or in a fish-ing ground called the Mud Hole, which lies south of Scotland and Ambrose lightships and is about fifteen miles long and five to ten miles wide. The Mud Hole is the upper part of the Old Hudson River Canyon, which was the bed of the river twenty thousand years ago, when the river flowed a hundred and twenty-five miles past what is now Sandy Hook before it reached the ocean. The draggers catch lower-depth and bottom feeders, chiefly whiting, butterfish, ling, cod, porgy, fluke, and flounder. They go out around 4 A.M. and return around 4 P.M., and their catches are picked up by trucks and taken to Fulton Market.

Some baymen set lines of lobster pots. In days gone by, there was a bountiful stock of lobsters in the harbor. Between 1915 and 1920, owing to pollution and overfishing and the bootlegging of berries, which are egg-carrying lobsters, and shorts and crickets, which are undersized lobsters, the stock began dwindling at a rapid rate. As late as 1920, forty-five lobstermen were still working the Upper Bay, the Narrows, and the Lower Bay. They ran out of seven inlets in Brooklyn and Staten Island, and their buoys dipped and danced all the way from the Statue of Liberty to the Hook. Every year in the twenties, a few of them either dropped out for good or bought bigger boats and forsook the bays and started setting pots out beyond the three-mile limit, in the harbor approaches. By 1930, only one lobsterman of any importance, Sandy Cuthbert, of Prince's Bay, continued to work the bays. In the fall of that year, at the close of the season, Mr. Cuthbert took up his pots—

he had two hundred and fifty—and stacked them on the bank of Lemon Creek, an inlet of Prince's Bay, and went into the rowboat-renting and fish-bait business. His pots are still there, rotting; generations of morning-glory and wild-hop vines are raveled in their slats and hold them together. During the thirties and forties, the lobsters began coming back, and divers say that now there are quite a few nests in the Upper Bay and many nests in the Lower Bay. However, they are still too scarce and scattered to be profitable. Sometimes, while repairing cables or pipelines on the bottom in parts of the Lower Bay where the water is clear and the visiblity is good, divers turn over rocks and pieces of waterlogged driftwood and lobsters scuttle out and the divers pick them up and put them in the tool sacks hooked to their belts.

At present, there are nine lobster boats working out of the harbor—six out of Plumb Beach; two out of Ulmer Park, on Gravesend Bay; and one out of Coney Island Creek. They are of the sea-skiff type. They range from twenty-six to twenty-eight feet, they are equipped with gasoline engines that are strong enough for much bigger boats, and, except for canvas spray hoods, they are open to the weather. The men on these boats are Scandinavians and Italians. They set their pots in a section of the Mud Hole southeast of Ambrose Lightship where the water in most places is over a hundred feet deep. They use the trawl method, in which the pots are hung at intervals from thick, tarred lines half a mile long; as a rule, thirty-five pots are hung from each line. The lines are buoyed at both ends with bundles of old, discarded ferryboat life preservers, which the lobstermen buy from a ship chandler in Fulton Market, who buys them from the Department of Marine and Aviation. Once a day, the lines are lifted, and each pot is pulled up and emptied of lobsters and chewed-up bait and stray crabs and fish, and rebaited with three or four dead mossbunkers. The coastwise and South American shipping lanes cross the lobster grounds in the Mud Hole, and every now and then a ship plows into a line and tears it loose from its buoys. Dump scows with rubbish from the city sometimes unload on the grounds and foul the lines and bury the pots. Mud Hole lobsters are as good as Maine lobsters; they can't be told apart. Some are sold to knowledgeable Brooklyn housewives who drive down to the piers in the middle of the afternoon, when the boats come in, and take their pick, but most are sold to Brooklyn restaurants. A boat working seven lines, which is the average, often comes in with around two hundred and fifty pounds.

A good many baymen work on public fishing boats that take sports fishermen out to fishing grounds in the harbor, in the harbor approaches, and along the Jersey coast. These boats are of two types—charter and party. Charter boats are cabin cruisers that may be hired on a daily or weekly basis. They are used for going after roaming surface feeders, big and small. Most of them are equipped with fighting chairs, fish hoists, and other contrivances for big-game fishing. They go out in the Lower Bay, Sandy Hook Bay, and Raritan Bay for striped bass, bluefish, and mackerel, and they go out to the Mud Hole and the Jersey grounds for tuna, albacore, bonito, and skipjack. They carry a captain and a mate, who baits and gaffs. Great Kills, which has fifteen boats, and Prince's Bay, which has eight, are the principal charter-boat ports in the harbor.

Party boats, also called open boats, are bigger boats, which operate on regular schedules and are open to anyone who has the fare; it varies from three and a half to five dollars a day. Sheepshead Bay is the principal party-boat port. It has over fifty boats. All of them leave from Emmons Avenue, which many people consider the most attractive waterfront street in the city. Emmons is a wide street, with a row of fluttery-leaved plane trees down the middle of it, that runs along the north shore of the bay. It smells of the sea, and of beer and broiled fish. On one side of it, for a dozen blocks, are bar-and-grills, seafood restaurants, clam stands, diners, pizza parlors, tackle and boat-gear stores, and fish markets, one of which has a cynical sign in its show window that says, "CATCH YOUR FISH ON THE NEVER-FAIL BANKS. USE A SILVER HOOK." The party-boat piers—there are ten of them, and they are long and roomy—jut out diagonally from the other side. Retired men from all over Brooklyn come down to the piers by bus and subway on sunny days and sit on the string-pieces and watch the boats go out, and rejuvenate their lungs with the brine in the air, and fish for blue-claw crabs with collapsible wirework traps, and quarrel with each other over the gulls; some bring paper bags of table scraps from home and feed the gulls and coo at them, and some despise the gulls and shoo them away and would wring their necks if they could get their hands on them. Among the boats in the Sheepshead Bay fleet are stripped-down draggers, converted yachts, and converted subchasers from both World Wars. The majority carry a captain and a mate and take around thirty passengers; the old sub-chasers carry a captain, a mate, an engineer, a cook, and a deckhand and take up to a hundred and ten passengers. Some have battered iceboxes on their decks and sell beer and pop and sandwiches, and some have galleys and sell hot meals. Some have conventional fishing-boat names, such as the *Sea Pigeon,* the *Dorothy B,* and the *Carrie D II,* and some have strutty names, such as the *Atomic,* the *Rocket,* and the *Glory.* Most of them leave at 5, 6, 7, 8, 9, or 10 A.M. and stay out the better part of the day. The passengers bring their own tackle, and fish over the rails. Bait is supplied by the boats; it is included in the fare. In most seasons, for most species, shucked and cut-up skimmer clams are used. These are big, coarse, golden-meated ocean clams. Cut-up fish, live fish, fiddler crabs, calico crabs, sand worms, and blood worms are also used. There are two dozen baymen in Sheepshead Bay who dig, dredge, net, and trap bait. They deliver it to three bait barges moored in the bay, and the barge-keepers put it into shape and sell it to the party boats by the tubful. For five weeks or so in the spring and for five weeks or so in the fall, during the mackerel migrations, the party boats go out and find schools of mackerel and anchor in the midst of them. The rest of the year, they go out and anchor over wrecks, reefs, scow dumps, and shellfish beds, where cod, ling, porgy, fluke, flounder, sea bass, blackfish, and other bottom feeders congregate.

There are many wrecks—maybe a hundred, maybe twice that; no one knows how many—lying on the bottom in the harbor approaches. Some are intact and some are broken up. Some are out in the Old Hudson River Canyon, with over two hundred feet of water on top of them. Some are close to shore, in depths of only twenty to thirty feet; around noon, on unusually clear, sunny fall days, when there is not much plankton in the water and the turbidity is low, it is possible to see these and see schools of sea bass streaming in and out of holes in their hulls. The wrecks furnish shelter for fish. Furthermore, they are coated, inside and out, with a lush, furry growth made up of algae, sea moss, tube worms, barnacles, horse mussels, sea anemones, sea squirts, sea mice, sea snails, and scores of other organisms, all of which are food for fish. The most popular party boats are those whose captains can locate the fishiest wrecks and bridle them. Bridling is a maneuver in which, say the wreck lies north and south, the party boat goes in athwart it and drops one anchor to the east of it and another to the west of it, so that party boat and wreck lie crisscross. Held thus, the party boat can't be skewed about by the wind and tide, and the passengers fishing over both rails can always be sure that they are dropping their bait on the wreck, or inside it. Good party-boat captains, by taking bearings on landmarks and lightships and buoys, can locate and bridle anywhere from ten to thirty wrecks. A number of the wrecks are quite old; they disintegrate slowly. Three old ones, all sailing ships, lie close to each other near the riprap jetty at Rockaway Point, in the mouth of the harbor. The oldest of the three, the *Black Warrior* Wreck, which shelters tons of sea bass from June until November, went down in 1859. The name of the next oldest has been forgotten and she is called the Snow Wreck; a snow is a kind of square-rigged ship similar to a brig; she sank in 1886, or 1887. The third one is an Italian ship that sank in 1890 with a cargo of marble slabs; her name has also been forgotten and she is called the Tombstone Wreck, the Granite Wreck, or the Italian Wreck. Over to the east, off the Rockaways, there is another group of old ones. In this group, all within five miles of shore, are the steamship *Iberia,* which sank in a snowstorm in 1889, after colliding with the steamship *Umbria;* the Wire Wreck, a sailing ship that sank around 1895 while outbound with a cargo of bedsprings and other wire products; the *Boyle* Wreck, a tug that sank around 1900; and the East Wreck, three coal barges that snapped their tow in a storm in 1917 and settled on the bottom in an equilateral triangle. Several of these wrecks have been fished steadily for generations, and party-boat captains like to say that they would be worth salvaging just to get the metal in the hooks and sinkers that have been snagged on them.

There are stretches of reefy bottom in the harbor approaches that are almost as productive of fish as the wrecks, and for the same reasons. These stretches are easier to locate than the wrecks, and much easier to fish. All have been named. Some are natural rock ledges, and among these are the Shrewsbury Rocks, the Buoy Four Grounds, the Cholera Bank, the Klondike Banks, the Seventeen Fathoms, and the

Farms. Some are artificial ledges, consisting of debris from excavations and torn-down buildings that was transported from the city in scows and dumped. One such is the Subway Rocks, a ridge of underwater hills beginning four miles south of Ambrose Lightship and running south for several miles, that was made of rocks, bricks, concrete, asphalt, and earth excavated during the construction of the Eighth Avenue Subway. Another such is the New Grounds, or Doorknob Grounds, a stretch of bottom in the northwest corner of the Mud Hole that is used as a dump for slum-clearance projects. There are bricks and brownstone blocks and plaster and broken glass from hundreds upon hundreds of condemned tenements in the New Grounds. The ruins of the somber old red-brick houses in the Lung Block, which were torn down to make way for Knickerbocker Village, lie there. In the first half of the nineteenth century, these houses were occupied by well-to-do families; from around 1890 until around 1905, most of them were brothels for sailors; from around 1905 until they were torn down, in 1933, they were rented to the poorest of the poor, and the tuberculosis death rate was higher in that block than in any other block in the city. All the organisms that grow on wrecks grow on the hills of rubble and rubbish in the Subway Rocks and the New Grounds.

. . .

The comings and goings of the baymen are watched by a member of the staff of the Bureau of Marine Fisheries of the State Conservation Department. His name is Andrew E. Zimmer, his title is Shellfish Protector, and his job is to enforce the conservation laws relating to marine shellfish and finfish. Mr. Zimmer is a Staten Islander of German descent. He is muscular and barrel-chested and a bit above medium height. He is bald and he is getting jowly. The department issues him a uniform that closely resembles a state trooper's uniform, but he seldom wears it. On duty, he wears old, knockabout clothes, the same as a bayman. He carries a pair of binoculars and a .38 revolver. He is called Happy Zimmer by the baymen, some of whom grew up with him. He is a serious man, a good many things puzzle him, and he usually has a preoccupied look on his face; his nickname dates from boyhood and he has outgrown it. He was born in 1901 on a farm in New Springville, a truck-farming community on the inland edge of the tide marshes that lie along the Arthur Kill, on the western side of Staten Island. In the front yard of the farmhouse, his father ran a combined saloon and German-home-cooking restaurant, named Zimmer's, that attracted people from the villages around and about and from some of the Jersey towns across the kill. Picnics and clambakes and lodge outings were held in a willow grove on the farm. His father had been a vaudeville ventriloquist, and often performed at these affairs. Specialties of the restaurant were jellied eels, clam broth with butter in it, and pear conchs from the Lower Bay boiled and then pickled in a mixture of vinegar and spices and herbs. As a boy, Mr. Zimmer supplied the restaurant with eels he speared in eel holes in the marshes and with soft-shell clams that he dug in the flats along the kill. Until 1916, when the harbor beds were condemned, Prince's Bay oysters were sold from the barrel in the saloon side of the restaurant. Friday afternoons, he and his father would drive down to the Oyster Dock in Prince's Bay in the farm wagon and bring back three or four barrels of selects for the week-end trade. In 1915, after completing the eighth grade, Mr. Zimmer quit school to help his father in the restaurant. In 1924, he took charge of it. In his spare time, mainly by observation in the marshes, he became a good amateur naturalist. In 1930, he gave up the restaurant and went to work for the Conservation Department.

Mr. Zimmer patrols the harbor in a lumbering, rumbly old twenty-eight-foot sea skiff. It has no flag or markings and looks like any old lobster boat, but the baymen can spot it from a distance; they call it the State Boat. Some of Mr. Zimmer's duties are seasonal. From March 15th to June 15th, when pound-netting is allowed, he makes frequent visits to the nets at pull-up time and sees to it that the fishermen are keeping only the species they are licensed for. When the mossbunker seiners come into the harbor, he boards them and looks into their holds and satisfies himself that they are not taking food fishes along with the mossbunkers. Now and then during the lobstering season, he draws up alongside the lobster boats inbound from the grounds and inspects their catches for shorts. Several times a year, he bottles samples of the water in various parts of the harbor and sends them to the department's laboratory. His principal year-round duty is to patrol the shellfish beds. He runs down and arrests poachers on the polluted beds, and he keeps an eye on the clammers who work the legal beds in Raritan Bay. It is against the law to do any kind of clamming between sundown and sunup, and he spends many nights out on the beds. He is a self-sufficient man. He can anchor his skiff in the shadow of a cattail hassock in Jamaica Bay and, without ever getting especially bored, sit there the whole night through with an old blanket over his shoulders, listening and watching for poachers and looking at the stars and the off-and-on lights on airplanes and drinking coffee out of a thermos jug. The legal beds in New Jersey territory in the harbor have been overworked and are not as fertile as the legal beds in New York territory. In recent years, allured by high clam prices, some of the Jersey clammers have become pirates. They tantalize Mr. Zimmer. On dark nights, using Chris Craft cruisers, they cross the state line, which bisects Raritan Bay, and poach on the New York beds. When they hear the rumble of Mr. Zimmer's skiff, they flee for Jersey. Mr. Zimmer opens his throttle and goes after them, shouting at them to halt and sometimes firing his revolver over their heads, but their cruisers draw less water than his skiff and at the end of the chase they are usually able to shoot up into one of the shallow tide creeks between South Amboy and the Hook and lose him. Mr. Zimmer keeps his skiff in Prince's Bay. Prince's Bay has gone down as a port since his boyhood. Not a trace of the oyster-bedding business is left there. It has a clam dock, a charter-boat pier, and two boat-yards, and it has Sandy Cuthbert's rowboat livery and bait station, but its chief source of income is a factory that makes tools for dentists; the factory is on Dental Avenue. The old Prince's Bay Lighthouse still stands on a bluff above the village, but it is now a part of Mount Loretto, a Catholic home for children; it is used as a residence by the Monsignor and priests who run the home. The light has been taken down and supplanted by a life-size statue of the Virgin Mary. The Virgin's back is to the sea.

Once in a while, Mr. Zimmer spends a day patrolling the Staten Island tide marshes on foot. He feels drawn to the marshes and enjoys this part of his job most of all. A good many people wander about in the marshes and in the meadows and little woods with which they are studded. He is acquainted with scores of marsh wanderers. In the fall, old Italians come and get down on all fours and scrabble in the leaves and rot beneath the blackjack oaks, hunting for mushrooms. In the spring, they come again and pick dandelion sprouts for salads. In midsummer, they come again, this time with scap nets, and scoop tiny mud shrimp out of the tide ditches; they use them in a fried fish-and-shellfish dish called *frittura di pesce*. On summer afternoons, old women from the south-shore villages come to the fringes of the marshes. They pick herbs, they pick wild flowers, they pick wild grapes for jelly, and in the fresh-water creeks that empty into the salt-water creeks they pick watercress. In the fall, truck farmers come with scythes and cut salt hay. When the hay dries, they pack it around their cold frames to keep the frost out. Bird watchers and Indian-relic collectors come in all seasons. The relic collectors sift the mud on the banks of the tide ditches. Mr. Zimmer himself some-times finds arrowheads and stone net-sinkers on the ditchbanks. Once, he found several old English coins. In September or October, the rabbis and elders come. On Hoshanna Rabbah, the seventh day of the Festival of Succoth, an ancient fertility rite is still observed in a number of orthodox synagogues in the city. The worshipers who take part in the rite are given bunches of willow twigs; each bunch has seven twigs and each twig has seven leaves. After marching in procession seven times around the altar, chanting a litany, the worshipers shake the bunches or strike them against the altar until the leaves fall to the floor. The twigs must be cut from willows that grow beside water, the buds on the ends of the twigs must be unblemished, and the leaves must be green and flawless. For generations, most of the willow bunches have come from black willows and weeping willows in the Staten Island tide marshes. In the two or three days preceding Hoshanna Rabbah—it usually falls in the last week of September or the first or second week of October—rabbis and trusted elders go up and down the ditchbanks, most often in pairs, the rabbi scrutinizing twigs and cutting those that pass the test, and the elder trimming and bunching them and stowing them gently in brown-paper shopping bags.

There is much resident and migratory wildlife in the marshes. The most plentiful resident species are pheasants, crows, marsh hawks, black snakes, muskrats, opossums, rabbits, rats, and field mice. There is no open season on the pheasants, and they have become so bold that the truck farmers look upon them as pests. One can walk through the pokeweed and sumac and blue-bent grass on any of the meadow islands at any time and put up pair after pair of pheasants. At the head of a snaky creek in one of the loneliest of the marshes, there is an old rickama-rack of a dock that was built by rum-runners during prohibition. One morning, hiding behind this dock, waiting for some soft-shell-clam poachers to appear, Mr. Zimmer saw a hen pheasant walk across a strip of tide flat, followed by a brood of seventeen. At times, out in the marshes, Mr. Zimmer becomes depressed. The marshes are doomed. The city has begun to dump garbage on them. It has already filled in hundreds of acres with garbage. Eventually, it will fill in the whole area, and then the Department of Parks will undoubtedly build some proper parks out there, and put in some concrete highways and scatter some concrete benches about. The old south-shore secessionists—they want Staten Island to secede from New York and join New Jersey, and there are many of them—can sit on these benches and meditate and store up bile.

Mr. Zimmer is a friend of mine, and I sometimes go out on patrols with him. One cold, windy, spitty morning, we made a patrol of the polluted skimmer-clam beds in the ocean off Rockaway Beach. On the way back to Staten Island, he suggested that we stop in Sheepshead Bay and get some oyster stew to warm us up. We turned in to the bay and tied the skiff to the Harbor Police float and went across the street to Lundy's, the biggest and best of the Emmons Avenue seafood restaurants. We went into the oyster-bar side and took a table, and each of us ordered a double stew. Mr. Zimmer caught sight of a bayman named Leroy Poole, who was standing at the bar, bent over some oysters on the half shell. Mr. Poole is captain and owner of the party boat *Chinquapin.* Mr. Zimmer went over to the bar, and he and Mr. Poole shook hands and talked for a minute or two. When he returned, he said that Mr. Poole would join us as soon as he'd finished his oysters. He told the waiter to set another place and add another double stew to the order. "Do you know Roy?" Mr. Zimmer asked me. I said that I had often seen him around the party-boat piers but that I knew him only to speak to.

"Roy's a south-shore boy," Mr. Zimmer said. "His father was one of the biggest oyster-bedders in Prince's Bay—lost everything when they condemned the beds, and took a bookkeeping job in Fulton Market and died of a stroke in less than a year; died on the Staten Island ferry, on the way to work. After Roy finished grade school, one of his father's friends got him a job in the market, and he became a fish butcher. When the carcass of a three- or four-hundred-pound swordfish is cut into pieces that the retail trade can handle, it's about the same as dressing a steer, and

Roy had a knack for that type of work. He got to be an expert. When he cut up a swordfish, or a tuna, or a sturgeon, or a big West Coast halibut, he didn't waste a pound. Also, he was a good fillet man, and he could bone a shad quicker and cleaner than any man in the market. He made good money, but he wasn't happy. Every now and then, he'd quit the market for a year or so and work on one of the government dredges that dredge the sludge out of the ship channels in the harbor. He generally worked on a dredge named the *Goethals*. He made better pay in the market, but he liked to be out in the harbor. He switched back and forth between the market and the *Goethals* for years and years. Somewhere along the line, he got himself tattooed. He's got an oyster tattooed on the muscle of his right arm. That is, an oyster shell. On his left arm, he's got one of those tombstone tattoos—a tombstone with his initials on it and under his initials the date of his birth and under that a big blue question mark. Six or seven years ago, he turned up in Sheepshead Bay and bought the *Chinquapin*. Roy's a good captain, and a good man, but he's a little odd. He says so himself. He's a harbor nut. Most of the baymen, when they're standing around talking, they often talk about the bottom of the harbor, what's down there, but that's *all* Roy talks about. He's got the bottom of the harbor on the brain."

The waiter brought in the stews, and a moment

later Mr. Poole came over and sat down. He is a paunchy, red-haired, freckled man. His hair is thinning and the freckles on his scalp show through. He has drooping eyelids; they make his eyes look sleepy and sad. He remarked on the weather; he said he expected snow. Then he tasted his stew. It was too hot for him, and he put his spoon down. "I didn't rest so good last night," he said. "I had a dream. In this dream, a great earthquake had shook the world and had upset the sea level, and New York Harbor had been drained as dry as a bathtub when the plug is pulled. I was down on the bottom, poking around, looking things over. There were hundreds of ships of all kinds lying on their sides in the mud, and among them were some wormy old wrecks that went down long years ago, and there were rusty anchors down there and dunnage and driftwood and old hawsers and tugboat bumpers and baling wire and tin cans and bottles and stranded eels and a skeleton standing waist-deep in a barrel of cement that the barrel had rotted off of. The rats had left the piers and were down on the bottom, eating the eels, and the gulls were flopping about, jerking eels away from the rats. I came across an old wooden wreck all grown over with seaweed, an old, old Dutch wreck. She had a hole in her, and I pulled the seaweed away and looked in and I saw some chests in there that had money spilling out of them, and I tried my best to crawl in.

The dream was so strong that I crawled up under the headboard of the bed, trying to get my hands on the Dutch money, and I damn near scraped an ear off."

"Eat your stew, Roy," Mr. Zimmer said, "before it gets cold."

"Pass me the salt," said Mr. Poole. We ate in silence. It isn't easy to carry on a conversation while eating oyster stew. Mr. Poole finished first. He tilted his bowl and worked the last spoonful of the stew into his spoon. He swallowed it, and then he said, "Happy, you've studied the harbor charts a lot in your time. Where would you say is the deepest spot in the harbor?"

"Offhand," said Mr. Zimmer, "I just don't know."

"One of the deepest spots I know is a hole in the bed of the Hudson a little bit south of the George Washington Bridge," said Mr. Poole. "On the dredges, we called it the Gut. It's half full of miscellaneous junk. The city used to dump bargeloads of boulders in there, and any kind of heavy junk that wasn't worth salvaging. Private concerns dumped in there, too, years back, but it's against the harbor regulations now. During the worst part of the last war, when the dredges cleaned sludge out of the ship channel in the Hudson, they had the right to dump it in the Gut—save them from taking it out to sea. The old-timers say the Gut used to go down a hundred and eighty feet. The last sounding I heard, it was around ninety feet. I know where the shallowest spot in the harbor is. I've sounded it myself with a boat hook. It's a spot on Romer Shoal, out in the middle of the Lower Bay, that's only four feet deep at low tide."

"Oh, yes," said Mr. Zimmer. "I've seen it on the charts. It's called a lump."

"It's right on the edge of Ambrose Channel, the channel that the big liners use," continued Mr. Poole. "I told my mate I want him to take me out there someday when the *Queen Mary* is due to come upchannel, and leave me standing there with a flag in my hand."

"What in hell would you do that for?" asked Mr. Zimmer.

"I'd just like to," said Mr. Poole. "I'd like to wave the flag and make the people on the *Queen Mary* wonder what I was standing on—shoulder-deep, out there in the middle of the Lower Bay. I'd wear a top hat, and I'd smoke a big cigar. I'd like to see what would happen."

"I'll tell you what would happen," said Mr. Zimmer. "The wash from the *Queen Mary* would drown you. Did you think of that?"

"I thought of it," said Mr. Poole. "I didn't do it, did I?" He crumpled up his napkin and tossed it on the table. "Another queer spot in the harbor," he said, "is Potter's Field. It's in the East River, in between Williamsburg Bridge and Manhattan Bridge. The river makes a sharp bend there, an elbow. On an ebb tide, there's an eddy in the elbow that picks up anything loose coming downriver, afloat or submerged, and sweeps it into a stretch of backwater on the Brooklyn side. This backwater is called Wallabout Bay on charts; the men on the dredges call it Potter's Field. The eddy sweeps driftwood into the backwater. Also, it sweeps drownded bodies into there. As a rule, people that drown in the harbor in winter stay down until spring. When the water begins to get warm, gas forms in them and that makes them buoyant and they rise to the surface. Every year, without fail, on or about the fifteenth of April, bodies start showing up, and more of them show up in Potter's Field than any other place. In a couple of weeks or so, the Harbor Police always finds ten to two dozen over there— suicides, bastard babies, old barge captains that lost their balance out on a sleety night attending to towropes, now and then some gangster or other. The police launch that runs out of Pier A on the Battery—Launch One—goes over and takes them out of the water with a kind of dip-net contraption that the Police Department blacksmith made out of tire chains. I ride the Staten Island ferry a good deal, and I'm forever hearing the tourists remark how beautiful the harbor is, and I always wish they could see Potter's Field some mornings in April—either that or the Gowanus Canal in August, when the sludge bubbles are popping like whips; they'd get a brand-new idea how beautiful the harbor is."

"Oh, I don't know, Roy," said Mr. Zimmer. "They've stopped dumping garbage out in the harbor approaches, where the tide washes it right back, and they're putting in a lot of sewage-disposal plants. The water's getting cleaner every year."

"I've read that," said Mr. Poole, "and I've heard it. Only I don't believe it. Did you eat any shad last spring—Staten Island shad *or* Hudson River shad? They've still got that kerosene taste. It was worse last spring than it ever was. Also, have you been up the Gowanus Canal lately? On the dredges, they used to say that the smell in the Gowanus would make the flag on a mast hang limp in a high wind. They used to tell about a tug that was freshly painted yellow and made a run up the Gowanus and came out painted green. I was up there last summer, and I didn't notice any change."

"Seriously, Roy," said Mr. Zimmer, "don't you think the water's getting cleaner?"

"Of course it isn't," said Mr. Poole. "It's getting worse and worse. *Every*thing is getting worse *every*where. When I was young, I used to dream the time would come when we could bed oysters in the harbor again. Now I'm satisfied that that time will never come. I don't even worry about the pollution any more. My only hope, I hope they don't pollute the harbor with something a million times worse than pollution."

"Let's don't get on that subject," said Mr. Zimmer.

"Sometimes I'm walking along the street," continued Mr. Poole, "and I wonder why the people don't just stand still and throw their heads back and open their mouths and howl."

"Why?" asked Mr. Zimmer.

"I'll tell you why," said Mr. Poole. "On account of the God-damned craziness of everything."

"Oh, well," said Mr. Zimmer, glancing at the empty stew bowls, "we can still eat."

Mr. Poole grunted. He looked at his wristwatch. "Well," he said, "this ain't making me any money." He got up and put on his hat. "Thanks for the stew," he said. "I enjoyed it. My treat next time. Take care, all."

"That's right, Roy," said Mr. Zimmer. "You take care of yourself."

"Thanks again," said Mr. Poole. "Give my regards home. Take care. Take care. Take care."

(1951)

The Rats on the Waterfront

In New York City, as in all great seaports, rats abound. One is occasionally in their presence without being aware of it. In the whole city relatively few blocks are entirely free of them. They have diminished greatly in the last twenty-five years, but there still are millions here; some authorities believe that in the five boroughs there is a rat for every human being. During wars, the rat populations of seaports and ships always shoot up. A steady increase in shipboard rats began to be noticed in New York Harbor in the summer of 1940, less than a year after the war started in Europe. Rats and rat fleas in many foreign ports are at times infected with the plague, an extraordinarily ugly disease that occurs in several forms, of which the bubonic, the Black Death of the

Middle Ages, is the most common. Consequently, all ships that enter the harbor after touching at a foreign port are examined for rats or for signs of rat infestation by officials of the United States Public Health Service, who go out in cutters from a quarantine station on the Staten Island bank of the Narrows. If a ship appears to be excessively infested, it is anchored in one of the bays, its crew is taken off, and its holds and cabins are fumigated with a gas so poisonous that a whiff or two will quickly kill a man, let alone a rat. In 1939 the average number of rats killed in a fumigation was 12.4. In 1940 the average rose abruptly to 21, and two years later it reached 32.1. In 1943, furthermore, rats infected with the plague bacteria, *Pasteurella pestis,* were discovered in the harbor for the first time since 1900. They were taken out of an old French tramp, the *Wyoming,* in from Casablanca, where the Black Death has been intermittent for centuries.

The biggest rat colonies in the city are found in run-down structures on or near the waterfront, especially in tenements, live-poultry markets, wholesale produce markets, slaughterhouses, warehouses, stables, and garages. They also turn up in more surprising places. Department of Health inspectors have found their claw and tail tracks in the basements of some of the best restaurants in the city. A few weeks ago, in the basement and sub-basement of a good old hotel in the East Forties, a crew of exterminators trapped two hundred and thirty-six in three nights. Many live in crannies in the subways; in the early-morning hours, during the long lulls between trains, they climb to the platforms and forage among the candy-bar wrappers and peanut hulls. There are old rat paths beneath the benches in at least two ferry sheds. In the spring and summer, multitudes of one species, the brown rat, live in twisting, many-chambered burrows in vacant lots and parks. There are great colonies of this kind of rat in Central Park. After the first cold snap they begin to migrate, hunting for warm basements. Packs have been seen on autumn nights scuttering across the boulevards and trans-verses in the Park and across Fifth Avenue and across Central Park West. All through October and Novem-ber, exterminating firms get frantic calls from the superintendents of many of the older apartment houses on the avenues and streets adjacent to the Park; the majority of the newer houses were rat-proofed when built. The rats come out by twos and threes in some side streets in the theatrical district practically every morning around four-thirty. The scow-shaped trucks that collect kitchen scraps from restaurants, night clubs, and saloons all over Manhattan for pig farms and soap factories in New Jersey roll into these streets at that time. Shortly after the trucks have made their pick-ups, if no people are stirring, the rats appear and search for dropped scraps; they seem to pop out of the air.

The rats of New York are quicker-witted than those on farms, and they can outthink any man who has not made a study of their habits. Even so, they spend most of their lives in a state of extreme anxiety, the black rats dreading the brown and both species dreading human beings. Away from their nests, they are usually on the edge of hysteria. They will bite babies (now and then, they bite one to death), and they will bite sleeping adults, but ordinarily they flee from people. If hemmed in, and sometimes if too suddenly come upon, they will attack. They fight savagely and blindly, in the manner of mad dogs; they bare their teeth and leap about every which way, snarling and snapping and clawing the air. A full-grown black rat, when desperate, can jump three feet horizontally and make a vertical leap of two feet two inches, and a brown rat is nearly as spry. They are greatly feared by firemen. One of the hazards of fighting a fire in a junk shop or in an old warehouse is the crazed rats. It is dangerous to poke at them. They are able to run right up a cane or a broomstick and inflict deep, gashlike bites on their assailant's hands. A month or so ago, in broad daylight, on the street in front of a riding academy on the West Side, a stableboy tried to kill a rat with a mop; it darted up the mop handle and tore the thumbnail off the boy's left hand. This happening was unusual chiefly in that the rat was foraging in the open in the daytime. As a rule, New York rats are nocturnal. They rove in the streets in many neighborhoods, but only after the sun has set. They steal along as quietly as spooks in the shadows close to the building line, or in the gutters, peering this way and that, sniffing, quivering, conscious every moment of all that is going on around them. They are least cautious in the two or three hours before dawn, and they are encountered most often by milkmen, night watchmen, scrubwomen, policemen, and other people who are regularly abroad in those hours. The average person rarely sees one. When he does, it is a disquieting experience. Anyone who has been confronted by a rat in the bleakness of a Manhattan dawn and has seen it whirl and slink away, its claws rasping against the pavement, thereafter understands fully why this beast has been for centuries a symbol of the Judas and the stool pigeon, of soullessness in general. Veteran exterminators say that even they are unable to be calm around rats. "I've been in this business thirty-one years and I must've seen fifty thousand rats, but I've never got accustomed to the look of them," one elderly exterminator said recently. "Every time I see one my heart sinks and I get the belly flutters." In alcoholic wards the rat is the animal that most frequently appears in the visual hallucinations of patients with delirium tremens. In these wards, in fact, the D.T.'s are often referred to as "seeing the rat."

There are three kinds of rats in the city—the brown *(Rattus norvegicus),* which is also known as the house, gray, sewer, or Norway rat; the black *(Rattus rattus),* which is also known as the ship or English rat; and the Alexandrian *(Rattus rattus alexandrinus),* which is also known as the roof or Egyptian rat and is a variety of the black rat. In recent years they have been killed here in the approximate proportion of ninety brown to nine black and one Alexandrian. The brown is hostile to the other kinds; it usually attacks them on sight. It kills them by biting their throats or by clawing them to pieces, and, if hungry, it eats them.

The behavior and some of the characteristics of the three kinds are dissimilar, but all are exceedingly destructive, all are hard to exterminate, all are monstrously procreative, all are badly flea-bitten, and all are able to carry a number of agonizing diseases. Among these diseases, in addition to the plague, are a form of typhus fever called Brill's disease, which is quite common in several ratty ports in the South; spirochetal jaundice, rat-bite fever, trichinosis, and tularemia. The plague is the worst. Human beings develop it in from two to five days after they have been bitten by a flea that has fed on the blood of a plague-infected rat. The onset is sudden, and the classic symptoms are complete exhaustion, mental confusion, and black, intensely painful swellings (called buboes) of the lymph glands in the groin and under the arms. The mortality is high. The rats of New York are all ridden with a flea, the *Xenopsylla cheopis,* which is by far the most frequent transmitting agent of the plague. Several surveys of the prevalence in the city of the *cheopis* have been made by Benjamin E. Holsendorf, a consultant on the staff of the Department of Health. Mr. Holsendorf, an elderly Virginian, is a retired Passed Assistant Pharmacist in the Public Health Service and an international authority on the ratproofing of ships and buildings. He recently supervised the trapping of many thousands of rats in the area between Thirty-third Street and the bottom of Manhattan, and found that these rats had an average of eight *cheopis* fleas on them. "Some of these rats had three fleas, some had fifteen, and some had forty," Mr. Holsendorf says, "and one old rat had hundreds on him; his left hind leg was missing—probably lost it in a trap, probably gnawed it off himself—and he'd take a tumble every time he tried to scratch. However, the average was eight. None of these fleas were plague-infected, of course. I don't care to generalize about this, but I will say that if just one plague-infested rat got ashore from a ship at a New York dock and roamed for only a few hours among our local, uninfected rats, the resulting situation might be, to say the least, quite sinister."

Rats are almost as fecund as germs. In New York, under fair conditions, they bear from three to five times a year, in litters of from five to twenty-two. There is a record of seven litters in seven months from a single captured pair. The period of gestation is between twenty-one and twenty-five days. They grow rapidly and are able to breed when four months old. They live to be three or four years old, although now and then one may live somewhat longer; a rat at four is older than a man at ninety. "Rats that survive to the age of four are the wisest and the most cynical beasts on earth," one exterminator says. "A trap means nothing to them, no matter how skillfully set. They just kick it around until it snaps; then they eat the bait. And they can detect poisoned bait a yard off. I believe some of them can read." In fighting the rat, exterminating companies use a wide variety of traps, gases, and poisons. There are about three hundred of these companies in the city, ranging in size from hole-in-the-wall, boss-and-a-helper outfits to corporations with whole floors in midtown office buildings, large laboratories, and staffs of carefully trained employees, many of whom have scientific degrees. One of the largest is the Guarantee Exterminating Company ("America's Pied Piper"), at 500 Fifth Avenue. Among its clients are hospitals, steamship lines, railroad terminals, department stores, office buildings, hotels, and apartment houses. Its head is E. R. Jennings, a second-generation exterminator; his father started the business in Chicago, in 1888. Mr. Jennings says that the most effective rat traps are the old-fashioned snap or break-back ones and a thing called the glueboard.

"We swear by the glueboard," he says. "It's simply a composition shingle smeared on one side with a thick, strong, black glue. We developed this glue twenty-five years ago and it's probably the stickiest stuff known to man. It has been widely copied in the trade and is used all over. The shingle is pliable. It can be laid flat on the floor or bent around a pipe. We place them on rat runs—the paths rats customarily travel on—and that's where skill comes in; you have to be an expert to locate the rat runs. We lay bait around the boards. If any part of the animal touches a board, he's done for. When he tries to pull away, he gets himself firmly caught in the glue. The more he struggles, the more firmly he's caught. Next morning the rat, glueboard and all, is picked up with tongs and burned. We used to bait with ground beef, canned salmon, and cheese, but we did some experimenting with many other foods and discovered that peanut butter is an extremely effective rat bait. Rats have to be trapped, poisoned, or gassed. Cats, if they're hungry enough, will kill rats, but you can't really depend on them—in many cases, they're able to keep the number of rats down, but they're seldom able to exterminate them.

"Insects, particularly cockroaches and bedbugs, are the Number One exterminating problem in New York. Rats come next. Then mice. Perhaps I shouldn't tell this, but most good exterminators despise rat jobs because they know that exterminating by itself is ineffective. You can kill all the rats in a building on a Monday and come back on a Wednesday and find it crawling with them. The only way rats can be kept out is to ratproof the building from sub-basement to skylight. It's an architectural problem; you have to build them out. Killing them off periodically is a waste of time. We refuse to take a rat job unless the owner or tenant promises to stop up every hole and crack through which rats can get in, and seal up or eliminate any spaces inside the building in which they can nest. That may sound like cutting our own throats, but don't worry: insects are here to stay and we'll always have more work than we can do. Twenty-five years ago there were easily two rats for every human being in the city. They gradually decreased to half that, for many reasons. Better sanitary conditions in general is one reason. Fewer horses and fewer stables is another. The improved packaging of foods helped a lot. An increase in the power of the Department of Health is an important reason. Nowadays, if a health inspector finds rat tracks in a grocery or a restaurant, all he has to do is issue a warning; if things aren't cleaned up in a hurry, he can slap on a violation and make it stick. The most important reason, however, is the modern construction of buildings and the widespread use of concrete. It's almost impossible for a rat to get inside some of the newer apartment houses and office buildings in the city. If he gets in, there's no place for him to hide and breed."

None of the rats in New York are indigenous to this country. The black rat has been here longest. Its homeland is India. It spread to Europe in the Middle Ages along trade routes, and historians are quite sure that it was brought to America by the first ships that came here. It is found in every seaport in the United States, and inland chiefly in the Gulf States. It has bluish-black fur, a pointed nose, and big ears. It is cleaner and not as fierce as the brown rat but more suspicious and harder to trap. It is an acrobatic beast. It can rapidly climb a drapery, a perpendicular drain or steam-heat pipe, an elevator cable, or a telephone or electric wire. It can gnaw a hole in a ceiling while clinging to an electric wire. It can run fleetly on a taut wire, or on a rope whether slack or taut. It uses its tail, which is slightly longer than its body, to maintain balance. It nests in attics, ceilings, and hollow walls, and in the superstructures of piers, away from its enemy, the ground-loving brown rat. Not all piers are infested; a few of the newer ones, which are made of concrete, have none at all. It keeps close to the waterfront, and until recently was rarely come across in the interior of the city. Whenever possible, it goes aboard ships to live. While docked here, all ships are required to keep three-foot metal disks, called rat guards, set on their hawsers and mooring cables. These guards sometimes get out of whack—a strong wind may tilt them, for example—and then a black or an Alexandrian can easily clamber over them. Occasionally a rat will walk right up or down a gangplank. It is almost impossible to keep a ship entirely free of them. Some famous ships are notoriously ratty. One beautiful liner—it was in the round-the-world cruise service before the war—once came in with two hundred and fifty aboard. Public Health Service officials look upon a medium-sized ship with twenty as excessively infested. The record for New York Harbor is held by a freighter that came in from an Oriental port with six hundred, all blacks and Alexandrians. The black and the Alexandrian are very much alike, and the untrained eye cannot tell them apart. The Alexandrian is frequently found on ships from Mediterranean ports. It is a native of Egypt, and no one seems to know, even approximately, when it first appeared in this country. It has never been able to get more than a toehold in New York, but it is abundant in some Southern and Gulf ports.

The brown rat, the *R. norvegicus,* originated somewhere in Central Asia, began to migrate westward early in the eighteenth century, and reached England around 1730. Most authorities believe that it got to this country during the Revolutionary War. From ports all along the coast it went inland, hot on the heels of the early settlers, and now it thrives in every community and on practically every farm in the United States. Its spread was slowest in the high and dry regions of the West; it didn't reach Wyoming until 1919 and Montana until 1923. Its nose is blunt, and its ears are small and alert, and its eyes are sharp and shiny and joyless and resentful and accusing. Its fur is most often a grimy brown, but it may vary from a pepper-and-salt gray to nearly black. Partial albinos occasionally show up; the tame white rat, which is used as a laboratory animal and sometimes kept as a pet, is a sport derived from the brown.

In addition to being the most numerous, the brown rat is the dirtiest, the fiercest, and the biggest. "The untrained observer," a Public Health Service doctor remarked not long ago, "invariably spreads his hands wide apart when reporting the size of a rat he has seen, indicating that it was somewhat smaller than a stud horse but a whole lot bigger than a bulldog. They are big enough, God protect us, without exaggerating." The average length of adult brown rats is ten inches, not counting the tail, which averages seven inches. The average weight is three-quarters of a pound. Once in a while a much heavier one is trapped. One that weighed a pound and a half and measured twenty and a half inches overall (that is, counting the tail) was recently clubbed to death in a Manhattan brewery; brewery and distillery rats feed on mash and many become obese and clumsy. Some exterminators have maintained for years that the biggest rats in the country, perhaps in the world, are found in New York City, but biologists believe that this is just a notion, that they don't get any bigger in one city than they do in another. The black and the Alexandrian are about two-thirds the size of the brown.

The brown rat is distributed all over the five boroughs. It customarily nests at or below street level— under floors, in rubbishy basements, and in burrows. There are many brownstones and red-bricks, as well as many commercial structures, in the city that have basements or sub-basements with dirt floors; these places are rat heavens. The brown rat can burrow into the hardest soil, even tightly packed clay, and it can tunnel through the kind of cheap mortar that is made of sand and lime. To get from one basement to another, it tunnels under party walls; slum-clearance workers frequently uncover a network of rat tunnels that link all the tenements in a block. Like the magpie, it steals and hoards small gadgets and coins. In nest chambers in a system of tunnels under a Chelsea tenement, workers recently found an empty lipstick tube, a religious medal, a skate key, a celluloid teething ring, a belt buckle, a shoehorn, a penny, a dime, and three quarters. Paper money is sometimes found. When the Civic Repertory Theatre was torn down, a nest constructed solely of dollar bills, seventeen in all, was discovered in a burrow. Exterminators believe that a high percentage of the fires that are classified as "of undetermined origin" are started by the brown rat. It starts them chiefly by gnawing the insulation off electric wires, causing short circuits. It often uses highly inflammable material in building nests. The majority of the nests in the neighborhood of a big garage, for example, will invariably be built of oily cotton rags.

The brown rat is as supple as rubber and it can squeeze and contort itself through openings half its size. It has strong jaws and long, curved incisors with sharp cutting edges. It can gnaw a notch big enough to accommodate its body in an oak plank, a slate shingle, or a sun-dried brick. Attracted by the sound of running water, it will gnaw into lead pipe. It cannot climb as skillfully as the black and the Alexandrian, it cannot jump as far, and it is not as fleet, but it is, for its size, a remarkable swimmer. A Harbor Police launch once came upon three brown rats, undoubtedly from New Jersey, in the middle of the Hudson; in an hour and twenty-five minutes, swimming against the wind in tossing water, they reached the pilings of one of the Barclay Street ferry slips, where the policemen shot them. The brown rat is an omnivorous scavenger, and it doesn't seem to care at all whether its food is fresh or spoiled. It will eat soap, oil paints, shoe leather, the bone of a bone-handled knife, the glue in a book binding, and the rubber in the insulation of telephone and electric wires. It can go for days without food, and it can obtain sufficient water by licking condensed moisture off metallic surfaces. All rats are vandals, but the brown is the most ruthless. It destroys far more than it actually consumes. Instead of completely eating a few potatoes, it takes a bite or two out of dozens. It will methodically ruin all the apples and pears in a grocery in a night. To get a small quantity of nesting material, it will cut great quantities of garments, rugs, upholstery, and books to tatters. In warehouses, it sometimes goes berserk. In a few hours a pack will rip holes in hundreds of sacks of flour, grain, coffee, and other foodstuffs, spilling and fouling the contents and making an overwhelming mess. Now and then, in live-poultry markets, a lust for blood seems to take hold of the brown rat. One night, in the poultry part of old Gansevoort Market, alongside the Hudson, a burrow of them bit the throats of over three hundred broilers and ate less than a dozen. Before this part of the market was abandoned, in 1942, the rats practically had charge of it. Some of them nested in the drawers of desks. When the drawers were pulled open, they leaped out, snarling.

So far, in the United States, the bubonic plague has been only a menace. From 1898 to 1923, 10,822,331 deaths caused by the plague were recorded in India alone; in the United States, in this period, there were fewer than three hundred deaths. The plague first occurred in this country in 1900, in the Chinatown of San Francisco. It is generally believed that the bacteria were brought in by infected rats that climbed to the docks from an old ship in the Far Eastern trade that caught afire while being unloaded. This epidemic killed a hundred and thirteen people and lasted until the end of 1903. The plague broke out again in 1907, a year after the earthquake. In the same year there was an epidemic in Seattle. There have been two epidemics in New Orleans—one in 1914 and one in 1919 and 1920—and there was one in Los Angeles in 1924 and 1925. Since then there have been only sporadic cases. However, there is a vast and ominous reservoir of plague infection in the rural rodents of the West.

During the first epidemic in San Francisco, many rats fled the city and infected field rodents, chiefly ground squirrels, in the suburbs. In 1934, thirty years later, Public Health Service biologists turned up the fact that the plague had slowly spread among burrowing animals—ground squirrels, prairie dogs, chipmunks, and others—as far east as New Mexico and Wyoming. Late last year it appeared fifty miles inside the western border of North Dakota. Public Health Service officials say that there is no reason to assume that the infection will not infiltrate into rodents of the Great Plains, cross the Mississippi, and show up in the East. Most of the diseased rodents inhabit thinly settled sections and come in contact with human beings infrequently. Even so, every year several people, usually hunters, are bitten by infected rodent fleas and come down with the plague. There is an ever-present possibility that a few infected rodents may stray from rural areas and communicate the disease to town and city rats. If the disease ever gets loose among city rats, epidemics among human beings are apt to follow.

There has never been an outbreak of the plague in New York. There have, however, been two narrow escapes. In 1900, plague-infected rats were found in ships in the harbor of New York, as well as in the harbors of San Francisco and Port Townsend, Washington. They got ashore only in San Francisco, causing the first Black Death epidemic in North America.

Plague rats were found in New York Harbor for the second time early in January of 1943. Among themselves, health officials refer to this discovery as "the *Wyoming* matter." The history of the *Wyoming* matter was told to me in 1944 by Dr. Robert Olesen, medical director of the New York Quarantine Station of the Public Health Service. Mr. Holsendorf sent me to see Dr. Olesen; they were colleagues years ago in the Public Health Service and are old friends. I saw Dr. Olesen in his office in an old, red-brick building overlooking the Narrows, in Rosebank, on Staten Island.

"The *Wyoming* matter has been one of the best-kept secrets in the history of the Public Health Service, and I'm proud of that," Dr. Olesen said, "but I agree with what Ben Holsendorf has been saying lately—there's no reason at all to keep it secret any longer. I'll tell you about it.

"First of all, I'd better explain how we inspect ships. Every ship in foreign trade that comes into the harbor is boarded by a party made up of a customs officer, an immigration officer, a plant-quarantine man from the Department of Agriculture, a Public Health doctor, and a sanitary inspector, whose main job is to determine the degree of rat infestation aboard. While the doctor is examining the crew and passengers for quarantinable diseases, the sanitary inspector goes through the ship looking for rat tracks, gnawings, droppings, and nests. Rats have a smell that is as distinctive as the smell of cats, although not as rank, and an experienced inspector can detect their presence that way. The inspector pays particular attention to ships that have touched at plague ports. There are quite a few of these ports right now; Suez had an outbreak the other day and was put on the list. After he's made his search, he reports to the doctor, who orders a fumigation if things look bad. If infestation is slight and if the ship comes from a clean port, the doctor probably won't insist on a fumigation. I won't give you any wartime figures, but in one peacetime month, for example, we inspected five hundred and sixty ships, found that a hundred and thirty-two were infested to some degree, and fumigated twenty-four, recovering eight hundred and ten rats.

"We've been short-handed since the war began, and most of our fumigating is done by a group of twenty-two Coast Guardsmen. They were assigned to us early in the war and we trained them to make rat inspections and fumigations. We use hydrocyanic gas, which is one of the most lethal of poisons. An infested ship is anchored and a fumigation party of four or five Coast Guardsmen goes aboard. First, they send the entire crew ashore, carefully checking them off one by one. Then one of the Coast Guardsmen goes through the ship, shouting, banging on bulkheads with a wrench, and making as much racket as possible. He shouts, 'Danger! Fumigation! Poison gas!' Then the Coast Guardsmen put on gas masks and toss some tear-gas bombs into the holds. That's to fetch out any stowaways who might be aboard. During the first months we used hydrocyanic, we killed a number of stowaways. A few weeks ago, in the hold of a South American freighter, the tear gas brought out eight weeping stowaways who had been hiding in an empty water tank. Two fellows in the crew had smuggled them aboard in Buenos Aires and had been feeding them. These fellows had kept their mouths shut and gone ashore, leaving the stowaways to be killed, for all they cared. When the Coast Guardsmen are satisfied a ship is empty of human beings, they seal the holds and cabins and open cans of hydrocyanic, liberating the gas. They even fumigate the lifeboats; rats often hide in them. After a certain number of hours—ten for a medium-sized ship—the holds are opened and aired out, and the Coast Guardsmen go below and search for dead rats. The rats are dropped in wax-paper bags and brought to a laboratory in the basement here. They are combed for fleas. The fleas are pounded in a mortar, put into a solution, and injected into guinea pigs. Then the rats are autopsied, and bits of livers and spleens are snipped out and pounded up. These are also put into a solution and injected into guinea pigs. If the fleas or the rats are infected, the pigs sicken and die. We began this work in 1921, and for twenty-two years we injected scores of generations of pigs with the fleas and livers and spleens of rats from practically every port in the world without turning up a single Black Death germ. We didn't want to find any, to be sure, but there were days when we couldn't help but look upon our work as routine and futile.

"Now then, late in the evening of January 10, 1943, the French freighter *Wyoming* arrived from Casablanca, North Africa, with a miscellaneous cargo, mainly wine and tobacco. A big convoy came in that evening, sixty or seventy ships, and we didn't get to the *Wyoming* until next day. Casablanca was on the plague list at that time; there had been an outbreak in December, shortly before the *Wyoming* sailed. The crew was carefully examined. No sign of illness. Then the captain brought out a deratization certificate stating that the ship had recently been fumigated—in Casablanca, if I remember correctly—and was free of rats; looking back, I feel sure the official who signed this certificate had been bribed. She was allowed to dock at Pier 34, Brooklyn, where she discharged some bags of mail. Next day she proceeded to Pier 84, Hudson River, and began discharging her cargo. Some rats were seen in her by longshoremen, and on January 13th we went over her and found evidence of infestation. She was allowed to continue unloading. On January 18th we fumigated her right at her dock and found twenty rats. We combed and autopsied the rats, and inoculated a guinea pig. Four days later the pig sickened and died. An autopsy indicated plague infection and cultures from its heart blood showed an oval organism which had all the characteristics of *Pasteurella pestis.* We made a broth of tissue from this pig and inoculated a second pig. It sickened and died. It was the Black Death, no doubt about it. We had found it in the harbor for the first time in forty-three years.

"In the meantime, the *Wyoming* had moved from the Hudson to Pier 25, Staten Island, for repairs. On January 29th we went aboard her, removed all excess dunnage and gear to the decks, and ripped open all the enclosed spaces in the holds; we were afraid the hydrocyanic hadn't penetrated to these spaces. Then we refumigated. Twelve more dead rats were found. On the same day we got in touch with Dr. Stebbins, the Commissioner of Health for the city, and told him about the situation. We were terribly apprehensive. The *Wyoming* had touched at piers in rat-infested sections in three boroughs and there was, of course, a distinct possibility that infected rats had got ashore and were at that moment wandering around the waterfront, coming in contact with local rats and exchanging fleas. Mr. Holsendorf, in his capacity as the Health Department's rat consultant, quickly got together some crews of trappers and put them to work setting break-back traps on the Brooklyn pier, the Manhattan pier, and the Staten Island pier, and in buildings in the vicinity of each pier. The trapping was done unobtrusively; we were afraid a newspaper might learn of the matter and start a plague scare. Early in February the first batch of rats was sent for autopsies to the laboratory of the Willard Parker Hospital, a hospital for contagious diseases, on the East River at Fifteenth Street. We sent them there, rather than bring them way down here to our laboratory, in order to get a report on them as quickly as possible. We waited for the report with considerable anxiety. It was negative on every rat, and we began to breathe easier. Mr. Holsendorf and his crews trapped from the end of January to the middle of May and the reports continued to come in negative. At the end of May we concluded that no *Wyoming* rats had got ashore, and that the city was safe."

(1944)

Mr. Hunter's Grave

When things get too much for me, I put a wild-flower book and a couple of sandwiches in my pockets and go down to the South Shore of Staten Island and wander around awhile in one of the old cemeteries down there. I go to the cemetery of the Woodrow Methodist Church on Woodrow Road in the Woodrow community, or to the cemetery of St. Luke's Episcopal Church on the Arthur Kill Road in the Rossville community, or to one on the Arthur Kill Road on the outskirts of Rossville that isn't used any longer and is known as the old Rossville burying ground. The South Shore is the most rural part of the island, and all of these cemeteries are bordered on at least two sides by woods. Scrub trees grow on some of the graves, and weeds and wild flowers grow on many of them. Here and there, in order to see the design on a gravestone, it is necessary to pull aside a tangle of vines. The older gravestones are made of slate, brownstone, and marble, and the designs on them—death's-heads, angels, hourglasses, hands pointing upward, recumbent lambs, anchors, lilies, weeping willows, and roses on broken stems—are beautifully carved. The names on the gravestones are mainly Dutch, such as Winant, Housman, Woglom, Decker, and Van Name, or Huguenot, such as Dissosway, Seguine, De Hart, Manee, and Sharrott, or English, such as Ross, Drake, Bush, Cole, and Clay. All of the old South Shore farming and oyster-planting families are represented, and members of half a dozen generations of some families lie side by side. In St. Luke's cemetery there is a huge old apple tree that drops a sprinkling of small, wormy, lopsided apples on the graves beneath it every September, and in the Woodrow Methodist cemetery there is a patch of wild strawberries. Invariably, for some reason I don't know and don't want to know, after I have spent an hour or so in one of these cemeteries, looking at gravestone designs and reading inscriptions and identifying wild flowers and scaring rabbits out of the weeds and reflecting on the end that awaits me and awaits us all, my spirits lift, I become quite cheerful, and then I go for a long walk. Sometimes I walk along the Arthur Kill, the tidal creek that separates Staten Island from New Jersey; to oldtime Staten Islanders, this is "the inside shore." Sometimes

I go over on the ocean side, and walk along Raritan Bay; this is "the outside shore." The interior of the South Shore is crisscrossed with back roads, and sometimes I walk along one of them, leaving it now and then to explore an old field or a swamp or a stretch of woods or a clay pit or an abandoned farm-house.

The back road that I know best is Bloomingdale Road. It is an old oystershell road that has been thinly paved with asphalt; the asphalt is cracked and pocked and rutted. It starts at the Arthur Kill, just below Rossville, runs inland for two and a half miles, gently uphill most of the way, and ends at Amboy Road in the Pleasant Plains community. In times past, it was lined with small farms that grew vegetables, berries, and fruit for Washington Market. During the depression, some of the farmers got discouraged and quit. Then, during the war, acid fumes from the stacks of smelting plants on the New Jersey side of the kill began to drift across and ruin crops, and others got discouraged and quit. Only three farms are left, and one of these is a goat farm. Many of the old fields have been taken over by sassafras, gray birch, blackjack oak, sumac, and other wasteland trees, and by reed grass, blue-bent grass, and poison ivy. In several fields, in the midst of this growth, are old woodpecker-ringed apple and pear trees, the remnants of orchards. I have great admiration for one of these trees, a pear of some old-fashioned variety whose name none of the remaining farmers can remember, and every time I go up Bloomingdale Road I jump a ditch and pick my way through a thicket of poison ivy and visit it. Its trunk is hollow and its bark is matted with lichens and it has only three live limbs, but in favorable years it still brings forth a few pears.

In the space of less than a quarter of a mile, midway in its length, Bloomingdale Road is joined at right angles by three other back roads—Woodrow Road, Clay Pit Road, and Sharrott's Road. Around the junctions of these roads, and on lanes leading off them, is a community that was something of a mystery to me until quite recently. It is a Negro community, and it consists of forty or fifty Southern-looking frame dwellings and a frame church. The church is painted white, and it has purple, green, and amber windowpanes. A sign over the door says, "AFRICAN METHODIST EPISCOPAL ZION." On one side of the church steps is a mock-orange bush, and on the other side is a Southern dooryard plant called Spanish bayonet, a kind of yucca. Five cedar trees grow in the churchyard. The majority of the dwellings appear to be between fifty and a hundred years old. Some are long and narrow, with a chimney at each end and a low porch across the front, and some are big and rambling, with wings and ells and lean-tos and front porches and side porches. Good pine lumber and good plain carpentry went into them, and it is obvious that attempts have been made to keep them up. Nevertheless, all but a few are beginning to look dilapidated. Some of the roofs sag, and banisters are missing on some of the porches, and a good many rotted-out clapboards have been replaced with new boards that don't match, or with strips of tin. The odd thing about the community is it usually has an empty look, as if everybody had locked up and gone off somewhere. In the summer, I have occasionally seen an old man or an old woman sitting on a porch, and I have occasionally seen children playing in a back yard, but I have seldom seen any young or middle-aged men or women sitting around, and I have often walked through the main part of the community, the part that is on Bloomingdale Road, without seeing a single soul.

For years, I kept intending to find out something about this community, and one afternoon several weeks ago, in St. Luke's cemetery in Rossville, an opportunity to do so presented itself.

I had been in the cemetery a couple of hours and was getting ready to leave when a weed caught my eye. It was a stringy weed, about a foot high, and it had small, lanceolate leaves and tiny white flowers and tiny seed pods, and it was growing on the grave of Rachel Dissosway, who died on April 7, 1802, "in the 27th Yr of her Age." I consulted my wild-flower book, and came to the conclusion that it was pepper-grass *(Lepidium virginicum),* and squatted down to take a closer look at it. "One of the characteristics of pep-pergrass," the wild-flower book said, "is that its seed pods are as hot as pepper when chewed." I deliber-ated on this for a minute or two, and then curiosity got the better of me and I stripped off some of the seed pods and started to put them in my mouth, and at just that moment I heard footsteps on the ceme-tery path and looked up and saw a man approach-ing, a middle-aged man in a black suit and a clerical collar. He came over to the grave and looked down at me.

"What in the world are you doing?" he asked.

I tossed the seed pods on the grave and got to my feet. "I'm studying wild flowers, I guess you might call it," I said. I introduced myself, and we shook hands, and he said that he was the rector of St. Luke's and that his name was Raymond E. Brock.

"I was trying to decide if the weed on this grave is peppergrass," I said.

Mr. Brock glanced at the weed and nodded. "Peppergrass," he said. "A very common weed in some parts of Staten Island."

"To tell you the truth," I said, "I like to look at wild flowers, and I've been studying them off and on for years, but I don't know much about them. I'm only just beginning to be able to identify them. It's mostly an excuse to get out and wander around."

"I've seen you from a distance several times wandering around over here in the cemetery," Mr. Brock said.

"I hope you don't mind," I said. "In New York City, the best places to look for wild flowers are old cemeteries and old churchyards."

"Oh, yes," said Mr. Brock, "I'm aware of that. In fact, I'll give you a tip. Are you familiar with the Negro community over on Bloomingdale Road?"

I said that I had walked through it many times, and had often wondered about it.

"The name of it is Sandy Ground," said Mr. Brock, "and it's a relic of the old Staten Island oyster-planting business. It was founded back before the Civil War by some free Negroes who came up here from the Eastern Shore of Maryland to work on the Staten Island oyster beds, and it used to be a flourishing community, a garden spot. Most of the people who live there now are descendants of the original free-Negro families, and most of them are related to each other by blood or marriage. Quite a few live in houses that were built by their grandfathers or great-grandfathers. On the outskirts of Sandy Ground, there's a dirt lane running off Bloomingdale Road that's called Crabtree Avenue, and down near the end of this lane is an old cemetery. It covers an acre and a half, maybe two acres, and it's owned by the African Methodist church in Sandy Ground, and the Sandy Ground families have been burying in it for a hundred years. In recent generations, the Sandy Grounders have had a tendency to kind of let things slip, and one of the things they've let slip is the cemetery. They haven't cleaned it off for years and years, and it's choked with weeds and scrub. Most of the gravestones are hidden. It's surrounded by woods and old fields, and you can't always tell where the cemetery ends and the woods begin. Part of it is sandy and part of it is loamy, part of it is dry and part of it is damp, some of it is shady and some of it gets the sun all day, and I'm pretty sure you can find just about every wild flower that grows on the South Shore somewhere in it. Not to speak of shrubs and herbs and ferns and vines. If I were you, I'd take a look at it."

A man carrying a long-handled shovel in one hand and a short-handled shovel in the other came into the cemetery and started up the main path. Mr. Brock waved at him, and called out, "Here I am, Joe. Stay where you are. I'll be with you in a minute." The man dropped his shovels.

"That's Mr. Damato, our gravedigger," said Mr. Brock. "We're having a burial in here tomorrow, and I came over to show him where to dig the grave.

You'll have to excuse me now. If you do decide to visit the cemetery in Sandy Ground, you should ask for permission. They might not want strangers wandering around in it. The man to speak to is Mr. George H. Hunter. He's chairman of the board of trustees of the African Methodist church. I know Mr. Hunter. He's eighty-seven years old, and he's one of those strong, self-contained old men you don't see much any more. He was a hard worker, and he retired only a few years ago, and he's fairly well-to-do. He's a widower, and he lives by himself and does his own cooking. He's got quite a reputation as a cook. His church used to put on clambakes to raise money, and they were such good clambakes they attracted people from all over this part of Staten Island, and he always had charge of them. On some matters, such as drinking and smoking, he's very disapproving and strict and stern, but he doesn't feel that way about eating; he approves of eating. He's a great Bible reader. He's read the Bible from cover to cover, time and time again. His health is good, and his memory is unusually good. He remembers the golden age of the oyster business on the South Shore, and he remembers its decline and fall, and he can look at any old field or tumble-down house between Rossville and Tottenville and tell you who owns it now and who owned it fifty years ago, and he knows who the people were who are buried out in the Sandy

Ground cemetery—how they lived and how they died, how much they left, and how their children turned out. Not that he'll necessarily tell you what he knows, or even a small part of it. If you can get him to go to the cemetery with you, ask him the local names of the weeds and wild flowers. He can tell you. His house is on Bloomingdale Road, right across from the church. It's the house with the lightning rods on it. Or you could call him on the phone. He's in the book."

I thanked Mr. Brock, and went straightway to a filling station on the Arthur Kill Road and telephoned Mr. Hunter. I told him I wanted to visit the Sandy Ground cemetery and look for wild flowers in it. "Go right ahead," he said. "Nobody'll stop you." I told him I also wanted to talk to him about Sandy Ground. "I can't see you today," he said. "I'm just leaving the house. An old lady I know is sick in bed, and I made her a lemon-meringue pie, and I'm going over and take it to her. Sit with her awhile. See if I can't cheer her up. You'll have to make it some other time, and you'd better make it soon. That cemetery is a disgrace, but it isn't going to be that way much longer. The board of trustees had a contractor look it over and make us a price how much he'd charge to go in there with a bulldozer and tear all that mess out by the roots. Clean it up good, and build us a road all the way through, with a turnaround at the farther end.

The way it is now, there's a road in there, but it's a narrow little road and it only goes halfway in, and sometimes the pallbearers have to carry the coffin quite a distance from the hearse to the grave. Also, it comes to a dead end, and the hearse has to back out, and if the driver isn't careful he's liable to back into a gravestone, or run against the bushes and briars and scratch up the paint on his hearse. As I said, a disgrace. The price the contractor made us was pretty steep, but we put it up to the congregation, and if he's willing to let us pay a reasonable amount down and the balance in installments, I think we're going ahead with it. Are you busy this coming Saturday afternoon?" I said that I didn't expect to be. "All right," he said, "I tell you what you do. If it's a nice day, come on down, and I'll walk over to the cemetery with you. Come around one o'clock. I've got some things to attend to Saturday morning, and I ought to be through by then."

Saturday turned out to be nice and sunny, and I went across on the ferry and took the Tottenville bus and got off in Rossville and walked up Bloomingdale Road to Sandy Ground. Remembering Mr. Brock's instructions, I looked for a house with lightning rods on it, and I had no trouble finding it. Mr. Hunter's house is fully equipped with lightning rods, the tips of which are ornamented with glass balls and metal arrows. It is a trim, square, shingle-sided, two-story-and-attic house. It has a front porch and a back porch, both screened. The front porch is shaded by a rambler rose growing on a trellis. I knocked on the frame of the screen door, and a bespectacled, elderly Negro man appeared in the hall. He had on a chef's apron, and his sleeves were rolled up. He was slightly below medium height, and lean and bald. Except for a wide, humorous mouth, his face was austere and a little forbidding, and his eyes were sad. I opened the door and asked, "Are you Mr. Hunter?" "Yes, yes, yes," he said. "Come on in, and close the door. Don't stand there and let the flies in. I hate flies. I despise them. I can't endure them." I followed him down the hall, past the parlor, past the dining room, and into the kitchen. There were three cake layers and a bowl of chocolate icing on the kitchen table.

"Sit down and make yourself at home," he said. "Let me put the icing on this cake, and then we'll walk over to the cemetery. Icing or frosting. I never knew which was right. I looked up icing in the dictionary one day, and it said 'Frosting for a cake.' So I looked up frosting, and it said 'Icing for a cake.' 'Ha!' I said. 'The dictionary man don't know, either.' The preacher at our church is a part-time preacher, and he doesn't live in Sandy Ground. He lives in Asbury Park, and runs a tailor shop during the week, and drives over here on Sundays. Reverend J. C. Ramsey, a Southern man, comes from Wadesboro, North Carolina. Most Sundays, he and his wife take Sunday dinner with me, and I always try to have something nice for them. After dinner, we sit around the table and drink Postum and discuss the Bible, and that's something I do enjoy. We discuss the prophecies in the Bible, and the warnings, and the promises—the promises of eternal life. And we discuss what I call the mysterious verses, the ones that if you could just understand them they might explain everything—why we're put here, why we're taken away—but they go down too deep; you study them over and over, and you go down as deep as you can, and you still don't touch bottom. 'Do you remember that verse in Relevation,' I say to Reverend Ramsey, 'where it says such and such?' And we discuss that awhile. And then he says to me, 'Do you remember that verse in Second Thessalonians, where it says so and so?' And we discuss that awhile. This Sunday, in addition to the preacher and his wife, I've got some other company coming. A gospel chorus from down South is going to sing at the church Sunday morning, a group of men and women from in and around Norfolk, Virginia, that call themselves the Union Gospel Chorus. They sing old hymns. Reverend Ramsey heard about them, and got into some correspondence with them. There's seven of them, and they're coming up on the bus today, and they'll spend the night in Asbury Park,

119

and tomorrow, after they sing, they're coming to my house for Sunday dinner. That'll be ten for dinner, including the preacher and his wife and me, and that's nothing. I have twenty to dinner sometimes, like at Thanksgiving, and do it all myself, and it doesn't bother me a bit. I'm going to give them chicken fricassee and dumplings for the main course. Soon as I finish this cake, I'll take you in the dining room and show you what else I'm going to give them. Did you have your lunch?"

"I had a sandwich and some coffee on the ferryboat coming over," I said.

"Now, you know, I like to do that," Mr. Hunter said. "I never go cross on the ferryboat without I step up to the lunch counter and buy a little something—a sandwich, or a piece of raisin cake. And then I sit by the window and eat it, and look at the tugboats go by, and the big boats, and the sea gulls, and the Statue of Liberty. Oh, my! It's such a pleasure to eat on a boat. Years and years ago, I was cook on a boat. When I was growing up in Sandy Ground, the mothers taught the boys to cook the same as the girls. The way they looked at it—you never know, it might come in handy. My mother was an unusually good cook, and she taught me the fundamentals, and I was just naturally good at it, and when I was seventeen or eighteen there was a fleet of fishing boats on Staten Island that went to Montauk and up around there and fished the codfish grounds, and I got a job cooking on one of them. It was a small boat, only five in the crew, and, the galley was just big enough for two pots and a pan and a stirring spoon and me. I was clumsy at first. Reach for something with my right hand and knock something else over with my left elbow. After a while, though, I got so good the captain of the biggest boat in the fleet heard about my cooking and tried to hire me away, but the men on my boat said if I left they'd leave, and my captain had been good to me, so I stayed. I was a fishing-boat cook for a year and a half, and then I quit and took up a different line of work altogether. I'll be through with this cake in just a minute. I make my icing thicker than most people do, and I put more on. Frosting. Speaking of wild flowers, do you know pokeweed when you see it?"

"Yes," I said.

"Did you ever eat it?"

"No," I said. "Isn't it supposed to be poisonous?"

"It's the root that's poisonous, the root and the berries. In the spring, when it first comes up, the young shoots above the root are good to eat. They taste like asparagus. The old women in Sandy Ground used to believe in eating pokeweed shoots, the old Southern women. They said it renewed your blood. My mother believed it. Every spring, she used to send me out in the woods to pick pokeweed shoots. And I believe it. So every spring, if I think about it,

I go pick some and cook them. It's not that I like them so much—in fact, they give me gas—but they remind me of the days gone by, they remind me of my mother. Now, away down here in the woods in this part of Staten Island, you might think you were fifteen miles on the other side of nowhere, but just a little ways up Arthur Kill Road, up near Arden Avenue, there's a bend in the road where you can sometimes see the tops of the skyscrapers in New York. Just the tallest skyscrapers, and just the tops of them. It has to be an extremely clear day. Even then, you might be able to see them one moment and the next moment they're gone. Right beside this bend in the road there's a little swamp, and the edge of this swamp is the best place I know to pick pokeweed. I went up there one morning this spring to pick some, but we had a late spring, if you remember, and the pokeweed hadn't come up. The fiddleheads were up, and golden club, and spring beauty, and skunk cabbage, and bluets, but no pokeweed. So I was looking here and looking there, and not noticing where I was stepping, and I made a misstep, and the next thing I knew I was up to my knees in mud. I floundered around in the mud a minute, getting my bearings, and then I happened to raise my head and look up, and suddenly I saw, away off in the distance, miles and miles away, the tops of the skyscrapers in New

York shining in the morning sun. I wasn't expecting it, and it was amazing. It was like a vision in the Bible."

Mr. Hunter smoothed the icing on top of the cake with a table knife, and stepped back and looked at it. "Well," he said, "I guess that does it." He placed a cover on the cake, and took off his apron. "I better wash my hands," he said. "If you want to see something pretty, step in the dining room and look on the sideboard." There was a walnut sideboard in the dining room, and it had been polished until it glinted. On it were two lemon-meringue pies, two coconut-custard pies, a pound cake, a marble cake, and a devil's-food cake. "Four pies and four cakes, counting the one I just finished," Mr. Hunter called out. "I made them all this morning. I also got some corn muffins put away, to eat with the chicken fricassee. That ought to hold them." Above the dining-room table, hanging from the ceiling, was an old-fashioned lampshade. It was as big as a parasol, and made of pink silk, and fringed and tasseled. On one wall, in a row, were three religious placards. They were printed in ornamental type, and they had floral borders. The first said "JESUS NEVER FAILS." The second said "NOT MY WILL BUT THINE BE DONE." The third said "THE HOUR IS COMING IN WHICH ALL THAT ARE IN THE GRAVES SHALL HEAR HIS VOICE, AND SHALL COME FORTH; THEY THAT HAVE DONE

GOOD, UNTO THE RESURRECTION OF LIFE AND THEY THAT HAVE DONE EVIL, UNTO THE RESURRECTION OF DAMNATION." On another wall was a framed certificate stating that George Henry Hunter was a life member of St. John's Lodge No. 29 of the Most Worshipful Prince Hall Grand Lodge of Free and Accepted Masons. While I was looking at this, Mr. Hunter came into the room. "I'm proud of that," he said. "There's several Negro Mason organizations, but Prince Hall is the biggest, and I've been a member since 1906. I joined the Masons the same year I built this house. Did you notice my floors?" I looked down. The floor boards were wide and made of some kind of honey-colored wood, and they were waxed and polished. "Virgin spruce," he said. "Six inches wide. Tongue and groove. Built to last. In my time, that was the idea, but in this day and time, that's not the idea. They've got more things nowadays—things, things, things; kitchen stoves you could put in the parlor just to look at, refrigerators so big they're all out of reason, cars that reach from here to Rossville—but they aren't built to last, they're built to wear out. And that's the way the people want it. It's immaterial to them how long a thing lasts. In fact, if it don't wear out quick enough, they beat it and bang it and kick it and jump up and down on it, so they can get a new one. Most of what you buy nowadays, the outside is everything, the inside don't mat-

ter. Like those tomatoes you buy at the store, and
they look so nice and shiny and red, and half the
time, when you get them home and slice them, all
that's inside is mush, red mush. And the people are
the same. You hardly ever see a son any more as good
as his father. Oh, he might be taller and stronger and
thicker in the shoulders, playing games at school and
all, but he can't stand as much. If he tried to lift
and pull the way the men of my generation used to
lift and pull, he'd be ruptured by noon—they'd be
making arrangements to operate. How'd I get started
talking this way? I'm tired, that's why. I been on my
feet all morning, and I better sit down a few minutes." He took a tablecloth from a drawer of the sideboard and shook it out and laid it gently over the
cakes and pies. "Let's go on the back porch," he said.

There were two wicker rocking chairs on the back
porch, and we sat down. Mr. Hunter yawned and
closed his eyes and slowly lowered his chin to his
chest. I looked at his back yard, in which there were
several rows of sweet potatoes, a row of tomatoes, a
weeping willow, and a feeding table for birds. Mr.
Hunter dozed for about five minutes, and then some
blue jays flew into the yard, shrieking, and they
aroused him. Pressing his elbows against the chair, he
sat up, and followed the jays with his eyes as they
swooped and swirled about the yard. When they flew

away, he laughed. "I enjoy birds," he said. "I enjoy their colors. I enjoy the noise they make, and the commotion. Even blue jays. Most mornings, I get up real early and go out in the yard and scatter bread crumbs and sunflower seeds on the feeding table, and then I sit up here on the porch and watch. Oh, it's nice out here in the early morning! Everything is so fresh. As my mother used to say, 'Every morning, the world anew.' Some mornings, I see a dozen different kinds of birds. There were redbirds all over the yard this morning, and a surprising number of brown thrashers and red-winged blackbirds. I see a good many I don't recognize; I do wish I knew their names. Every so often, a pair of pheasants land on the feeding table. Some of the old fields around here are full of them. I was picking some tomatoes the other day, and a pair of pheasants scuttled out from under the tomato bushes and flew up right in my face. Whoosh! Up goes the cock bird. A second later—whoosh! Up goes the hen bird. One of her wings brushed against me. I had my mind on something else, or I could've caught her. I better not get on the subject of birds, or I'll talk your ears off. You said on the phone you wanted to know something about Sandy Ground. What do you want to know? How it began?"

"Yes, sir," I said.

"Oysters!" said Mr. Hunter. "That's how it

began." There was a fly swatter on the floor beside
Mr. Hunter's chair, and a few feet in front of his chair
was an old kitchen table with a chipped enamel top.
He suddenly reached down and grabbed the swatter
and stood up and took a step toward the table, on
which a fly had lit. His shadow fell on the fly, and the
fly flew away. Mr. Hunter stared wildly into space for
several moments, looking for the fly and muttering
angrily, and then he sat back down, still holding the
swatter.

"It's hard to believe nowadays, the water's so
dirty," he continued, "but up until about the year
1800 there were tremendous big beds of natural-
growth oysters all around Staten Island—in the
Lower Bay, in the Arthur Kill, in the Kill van Kull.
Some of the richest beds of oysters in the entire
country were out in the lower part of the Lower Bay,
the part known as Raritan Bay. Most of them were
on shoals, under ten to twenty feet of water. They
were supposed to be public beds, open to anybody,
but they were mainly worked by Staten Islanders, and
the Staten Islanders considered they owned them.
Between 1800 and 1820, all but the very deepest of
these beds gradually petered out. They had been
raked and scraped until they weren't worth working
any more. But the Staten Islanders didn't give up.
What they did, they began to bring immature oysters
from other localities and put them on the best of the

old beds and leave them there until they reached market size, which took from one to four years, all according to how mature the oysters were to begin with. Then they'd rake them up, or tong them up, and load them on boats, and send them up the bay to the wholesalers in New York. They took great pains with these oysters. They cleaned the empty shells and bottom trash off the beds that they put them on, and they spread them out as evenly as possible. Handled this way, oysters grew faster than they did all scrouged together on natural beds. Also, they grew more uniform in size and shape. Also, they had a better flavor. Also, they brought higher prices, premium prices. The center of the business was the little town of Prince's Bay, over on the outside shore.

"At first, the Staten Islanders used sloops and bought their seed stock close by, in bays in New Jersey and Long Island, but the business grew very fast, and in a few years a good many of them were using schooners that could hold five thousand bushels and were making regular trips to Maryland and Virginia. Some went into inlets along the ocean side of the Eastern Shore, and some went into Chesapeake Bay. They bought from local oystermen who worked natural beds in the public domain, and they usually had to visit a whole string of little ports and landings before they got a load. At that time, there were quite a few free Negroes among the oystermen on the Eastern Shore, especially in Worcester County, Maryland, on the upper part of Chincoteague Bay, and the Staten Island captains occasionally hired gangs of them to make the trip North and help distribute the oysters on the beds. Now and then, a few would stay behind on Staten Island for a season or two and work on empty beds, cleaning them off and getting them ready for new seed stock. Late in the eighteen-thirties or early in the eighteen-forties, a number of these men left their homes in and around Snow Hill, Maryland, the county seat of Worcester County, and came up to Staten Island to live. They brought their families, and they settled over here in the Sandy Ground section. The land was cheap in Sandy Ground, and it was in easy walking distance of Prince's Bay, and a couple of Negro families were already living over here, a family named Jackson and a family named Henry. The records of our church go back to 1850, and they show the names of most of the original men from Snow Hill. Three of them were Purnells—Isaac Purnell, George Purnell, and Littleton Purnell. Two were Lambdens, spelled L-a-m-b-d-e-n, only their descendants changed the spelling to L-a-n-d-i-n—Landin. One was a Robbins, and one was a Bishop, and one was a Henman. The Robbins family died out or moved away many years ago, but Purnells, Landins, Bishops, and Henmans still live in Sandy Ground. They've always been the main Sandy Ground families. There's a man from Sandy Ground who works for a trucking concern in New York, drives trailer trucks, and he's driven through Maryland many times, and stopped in Snow Hill, and he says there's still people down there with these names, plenty of them, white and Negro. Especially Purnells and Bishops. Every second person you run into in Snow Hill, just about, he says, is either a Purnell or a Bishop, and there's one little crossroad town near Snow Hill that's named Bishop and another one that's named Bishopville. Through the years, other Negro families came to Sandy Ground and settled down and intermarried with the families from Snow Hill. Some came from the South, but the majority came from New York and New Jersey and other places in the North. Such as the Harris family, the Mangin family, the Fish family, the Williams family, the Finney family, and the Roach family."

All of a sudden, Mr. Hunter leaned forward in his chair as far as he could go and brought the fly swatter down on the table. This time, he killed the fly.

"I wasn't born in Sandy Ground myself," he continued. "I came here when I was a boy. My mother and my stepfather brought me here. Two or three of the original men from Snow Hill were still around then, and I knew them. They were old, old men. They were as old as I am now. And the widows of several others were still around. Two of those old widows lived near us, and they used to come to see my mother and sit by the kitchen range and talk and talk, and I used to like to listen to them. The main thing they talked about was the early days in Sandy Ground—how poor everybody had been, and how hard everybody had had to work, the men and the women. The men all worked by the day for the white oystermen in Prince's Bay. They went out in skiffs and anchored over the beds and stood up in the skiffs from sunup to sundown, raking oysters off the bottom with big old clawtoothed rakes that were made of iron and weighed fourteen pounds and had handles on them twenty-four feet long. The women all washed. They washed for white women in Prince's Bay and Rossville and Tottenville. And there wasn't a real house in the whole of Sandy Ground. Most of the families lived in one-room shacks with lean-tos for the children. In the summer, they ate what they grew in their gardens. In the winter, they ate oysters until they couldn't stand the sight of them.

"When I came here, early in the eighteen-eighties, that had all changed. By that time, Sandy Ground was really quite a prosperous little place. Most of the men were still breaking their backs raking oysters by the day, but several of them had saved their money and worked up to where they owned and operated pretty good-sized oyster sloops and didn't take orders from anybody. Old Mr. Dawson Landin was the first to own a sloop. He owned a forty-footer named the *Pacific*. He was the richest man in the settlement, and he took the lead in everything. Still and all, people liked him and looked up to him; most of us called him Uncle Daws. His brother, Robert Landin, owned a thirty-footer named the *Independence,* and Mr. Robert's son-in-law, Francis Henry, also owned a thirty-footer. His was named the *Fanny Fern.* And a few others owned sloops. There were still some places here and there in the Arthur Kill and the Kill van Kull where you could rake up natural-growth seed oysters if you spliced two rake handles together and went down deep enough, and that's what these men did. They sold the seed to the white oystermen, and they made out all right. In those days, the oyster business used oak baskets by the thousands, and some of the Sandy Ground men had got to be good basket-makers. They went into the woods around here and cut white-oak saplings and split them into strips and soaked the strips in water and wove them into bushel baskets that would last for years. Also, several of the men had become black-smiths. They made oyster rakes and repaired them, and did all kinds of ironwork for the boats.

"The population of Sandy Ground was bigger then than it is now, and the houses were newer and nicer-looking. Every family owned the house they lived in, and a little bit of land. Not much—an acre and a half, two acres, three acres. I guess Uncle Daws had the most, and he only had three and three-quarter acres. But what they had, they made every inch of it count. They raised a few pigs and chickens, and kept a cow, and had some fruit trees and grapevines, and planted a garden. They planted a lot of Southern stuff, such as butter beans and okra and sweet potatoes and mustard greens and collards and Jerusalem artichokes. There were flowers in every yard, and rose-bushes, and the old women exchanged seeds and bulbs and cuttings with each other. Back then, this was a big strawberry section. The soil in Sandy Ground is ideal for strawberries. All the white farmers along Bloomingdale Road grew them, and the people in Sandy Ground took it up; you can grow a lot of strawberries on an acre. In those days, a river steamer left New Brunswick, New Jersey, every morning, and came down the Raritan River and entered the Arthur Kill and made stops at Rossville and five or six other little towns on the kill, and then went on up to the city and docked at the foot of Barclay Street, right across from Washington Market. And early every morning during strawberry season the people would box up their strawberries and take them down to Rossville and put them on a steamer and send them off to market. They'd lay a couple of grape leaves on top of each box, and that would bring out the beauty of the berries, the green against the red. Staten Island strawberries had the reputation of being unusually good, the best on the market, and they brought fancy prices. Most of them went to the big New York hotels. Some of the families in Sandy Ground, strawberries were about as important to them as oysters. And every family put up a lot of stuff, not only garden stuff, but wild stuff—wild-grape jelly, and wild-plum jelly, and huckleberries. If it was a good huckleberry year, they'd put up enough huckleberries to make deep-dish pies all winter. And when they killed their hogs, they made link sausages and liver pudding and lard. Some of the old women even made soap. People looked after things in those days. They patched and mended and made do, and they kept their yards clean, and they burned their trash. And they taught their children how to conduct themselves. And they held their heads up; they were as good as anybody, and better than some. And they got along with each other; they knew each other's peculiarities and took them into consideration. Of course, this was an oyster town, and there was always an element that drank and carried on and didn't have any more moderation than the cats up the alley, but the great majority were good Christians who walked in the way of the Lord, and loved Him, and trusted Him, and kept His commandments. Everything in Sandy Ground revolved around the church. Every summer, we put up a tent in the churchyard and held a big camp meeting, a revival. We owned the tent. We could get three or four hundred people under it, sitting on sawhorse benches. We'd have visiting preachers, famous old-time African Methodist preachers, and they'd preach every night for a week. We'd invite the white oystermen to come and bring their families, and a lot of them would. Everybody was welcome. And once a year, to raise money for church upkeep, we'd put on an ox roast, what they call a barbecue nowadays. A Southern man named Steve Davis would do the roasting. There were tricks to it that only he knew. He'd dig a pit in the church-yard, and then a little off to one side he'd burn a pile of hickory logs until he had a big bed of red-hot coals, and then he'd fill the pit about half full of coals, and then he'd set some iron rods across the pit, and then he'd lay a couple of sides of beef on the rods and let them roast. Every now and then, he'd shovel some more coals into the pit, and then he'd turn the sides of beef and baste them with pepper sauce, or whatever it was he had in that bottle of his, and the beef would drip and sputter and sizzle, and the smoke from the hickory coals would flavor it to per-fection. People all over the South Shore would set aside that day and come to the African Methodist ox roast. All the big oyster captains in Prince's Bay would come. Captain Phil De Waters would come, and Captain Abraham Manee and Captain William Haughwout and Captain Peter Polworth and good old Captain George Newbury, and a dozen others. And we'd eat and laugh and joke with each other over who could hold the most.

"All through the eighties, and all through the nineties, and right on up to around 1910, that's the way it was in Sandy Ground. Then the water went bad. The oystermen had known for a long time that the water in the Lower Bay was getting dirty, and they used to talk about it, and worry about it, but they didn't have any idea how bad it was until around 1910, when reports began to circulate that cases of typhoid fever had been traced to the eating of Staten Island oysters. The oyster wholesalers in New York were the unseen powers in the Staten Island oyster business; they advanced the money to build boats and buy Southern seed stock. When the typhoid talk got started, most of them decided they didn't want to risk their money any more, and the business went into a decline, and then, in 1916, the Department of Health stepped in and condemned the beds, and that was that. The men in Sandy Ground had to scratch around and look for something else to do, and it wasn't easy. Mr. George Ed Henman got a job working on a garbage wagon for the city, and Mr. James McCoy became the janitor of a public school, and Mr. Jacob Finney went to work as a porter on Ellis

Island, and one did this and one did that. A lot of the life went out of the settlement, and a kind of don't-care attitude set in. The church was especially hard hit. Many of the young men and women moved away, and several whole families, and the membership went down. The men who owned oyster sloops had been the main support of the church, and they began to give dimes where they used to give dollars. Steve Davis died, and it turned out nobody else knew how to roast an ox, so we had to give up the ox roasts. For some years, we put on clambakes instead, and then clams got too dear, and we had to give up the clambakes.

"The way it is now, Sandy Ground is just a ghost of its former self. There's a disproportionate number of old people. A good many of the big old rambling houses that used to be full of children, there's only old men and old women living in them now. And you hardly ever see them. People don't sit on their porches in Sandy Ground as much as they used to, even old people, and they don't do much visiting. They sit inside, and keep to themselves, and listen to the radio or look at television. Also, in most of the families in Sandy Ground where the husband and wife are young or middle-aged, both of them go off to work. If there's children, a grandmother or an old aunt or some other relative stays home and looks after them. And they have to travel good long distances to get to their work. The women mainly work in hospitals, such as Sea View, the big TB hospital way up in the middle of the island, and I hate to think of the time they put in riding those rattly old Staten Island buses and standing at bus stops in all kinds of weather. The men mainly work in construction, or in factories across the kill in New Jersey. You hear their cars starting up early in the morning, and you hear them coming in late at night. They make eighty, ninety, a hundred a week, and they take all the over-time work they can get; they have to, to pay for those big cars and refrigerators and television sets. When-ever something new comes out, if one family gets one, the others can't rest until they get one too. And the only thing they pay cash for is candy bars. For all I know, they even buy them on the installment plan. It'll all end in a mess one of these days. The church has gone way down. People say come Sunday they're just too tired to stir. Most of the time, only a handful of the old reliables show up for Sunday-morning ser-vices, and we've completely given up Sunday-evening services. Oh, sometimes a wedding or a funeral will draw a crowd. As far as gardens, nobody in Sandy Ground plants a garden any more beyond some old woman might set out a few tomato plants and half the time she forgets about them and lets them wilt. As far as wild stuff, there's plenty of huckleberries in the woods around here, high-bush and low-bush, and oceans of blackberries, and I even know where there's some beach plums, but do you think anybody bothers with them? Oh, no!"

Mr. Hunter stood up. "I've rested long enough," he said. "Let's go on over to the cemetery." He went down the back steps, and I followed him. He looked under the porch and brought out a grub hoe and handed it to me. "We may need this," he said. "You take it, if you don't mind, and go on around to the front of the house. I'll go back inside and lock up, and I'll meet you out front in just a minute."

I went around to the front, and looked at the roses on the trellised bush beside the porch. They were lush pink roses. It was a hot afternoon, and when Mr. Hunter came out, I was surprised to see that he had put on a jacket, and a double-breasted jacket at that. He had also put on a black necktie and a black felt hat. They were undoubtedly his Sunday clothes, and he looked stiff and solemn in them.

"I was admiring your rosebush," I said.

"It does all right," said Mr. Hunter. "It's an old bush. When it was getting a start, I buried bones from the table around the roots of it, the way the old Southern women used to do. Bones are the best fertilizer in the world for rosebushes." He took the hoe and put it across his shoulder, and we started up Bloomingdale Road. We walked in the road; there are no sidewalks in Sandy Ground.

A little way up the road, we overtook an old man hobbling along on a cane. He and Mr. Hunter spoke to each other, and Mr. Hunter introduced me to him. "This is Mr. William E. Brown," Mr. Hunter said. "He's one of the old Sandy Ground oystermen. He's in his eighties, but he's younger than me. How are you, Mr. Brown?"

"I'm just hanging by a thread," said Mr. Brown.

"Is it as bad as that?" asked Mr. Hunter

"Oh, I'm all right," said Mr. Brown, "only for this numbness in my legs, and I've got cataracts and can't half see, and I had a dentist make me a set of teeth and he says they fit, but they don't, they slip, and I had double pneumonia last winter and the doctor gave me some drugs that addled me. And I'm still addled."

"This is the first I've seen you in quite a while," said Mr. Hunter.

"I stay to myself," said Mr. Brown. "I was never one to go to people's houses. They talk and talk, and you listen, you bound to listen, and half of it ain't true, and the next time they tell it, they say you said it."

"Well, nice to see you, Mr. Brown," said Mr. Hunter.

"Nice to see you, Mr. Hunter," said Mr. Brown. "Where you going?"

"Just taking a walk over to the cemetery," said Mr. Hunter.

"Well, you won't get in any trouble over there," said Mr. Brown.

We resumed our walk.

"Mr. Brown came to Sandy Ground when he was a boy, the same as I did," Mr. Hunter said. "He was born in Brooklyn, but his people were from the South."

"Were you born in the South, Mr. Hunter?" I asked.

"No, I wasn't," he said.

His face became grave, and we walked past three or four houses before he said any more.

"I wasn't," he finally said. "My mother was. To tell you the truth, my mother was born in slavery. Her name was Martha, Martha Jennings, and she was born in the year 1849. Jennings was the name of the man who owned her. He was a big farmer in the Shenandoah Valley in Virginia. He also owned my mother's mother, but he sold her when my mother was five years old, and my mother never saw or heard of her again. Her name was Hettie. We couldn't ever get much out of my mother about slavery days. She didn't like to talk about it, and she didn't like for us to talk about it. 'Let the dead bury the dead,' she used to say. Just before the Civil War, when my mother was eleven or twelve, the wife of the man who owned her went to Alexandria, Virginia, to spend the summer, and she took my mother along to attend to her children. Somehow or other, my mother got in with some people in Alexandria who helped her run away. Some antislavery people. She never said so in so many words, but I guess they put her on the Underground Railroad. Anyway, she wound up in what's now Ossining, New York, only then it was called the village of Sing Sing, and by and by she married my father. His name was Henry Hunter, and he was a hired man on an apple farm just outside Sing Sing. She had fifteen children by him, but only three—me, my brother William, and a girl named Hettie—lived past the age of fourteen; most of them died when they were babies. My father died around 1879, 1880, somewhere in there. A few months after he died, a man named Ephraim Purnell rented a room in our house. Purnell was an oysterman from Sandy Ground. He was a son of old man Littleton Purnell, one of the original men from Snow Hill. He had got into some trouble in Prince's Bay connected with stealing, and had been sent to Sing Sing Prison. After he served out his sentence, he decided he'd see if he could get a job in Sing Sing village and live there. My mother tried to help him, and ended up marrying him. He couldn't get a job up there, nobody would have him, so he brought my mother and me and William and Hettie down here to Sandy Ground and he went back to oystering."

We turned off Bloomingdale Road and entered Crabtree Avenue, which is a narrow dirt road lined on one side with sassafras trees and on the other with a straggly privet hedge.

"I didn't like my stepfather," Mr. Hunter continued. "I not only didn't like him, I despised him. He was a drunkard, a sot, and he mistreated my mother. From the time we landed in Sandy Ground, as small as I was, my main object in life was to support myself. I didn't want him supporting me. And I didn't want to go into the oyster business, because he was in it. I worked for a farmer down the road a few years—one of the Sharrotts that Sharrott's Road is named for. Then I cooked on a fishing boat. Then I became a hod carrier. Then something got into me, and I began to drink. I turned into a sot myself. After I had been drinking several years, I was standing in a grocery store in Rossville one day, and I saw my mother walk past outside on the street. I just caught a glimpse of her face through the store window as she walked past, and she didn't know anybody was looking at her, and she had a horrible hopeless look on her face. A week or so later, I knocked off work in the middle of the day and bought a bottle of whiskey, the way I sometimes did, and I went out in the woods between Rossville and Sandy Ground and sat down on a rock, and I was about as low in my mind as a man can be; I knew what whiskey was doing to me, and yet I couldn't stop drinking it. I tore the stamp off the bottle and pulled out the cork, and got ready to take a drink, and then I remembered the look on my mother's face, and a peculiar thing happened. The best way I can explain it, my gorge rose. I got mad at myself, and I got mad at the world. Instead of taking a drink, I poured the whiskey on the ground and smashed the bottle on the rock, and stood up and walked out of the woods. And I never drank another drop. I wanted to many a time, many and many a time, but I tightened my jaw against myself, and I stood it off. When I look back, I don't know how I did it, but I stood it off, I stood it off."

We walked on in silence for a few minutes, and then Mr. Hunter sighed and said, "Ah, well!"

"From being a hod carrier, I became a bricklayer," he continued, "but that wasn't as good as it sounds; bricklayers didn't make much in those days. And in 1896, when I was twenty-seven, I got married to my first wife. Her name was Celia Ann Finney, and she was the daughter of Mr. Jacob Finney, one of the oystermen. She was considered the prettiest girl in Sandy Ground, and the situation I was in, she had turned down a well-to-do young oysterman to marry me, a fellow with a sloop, and I knew everybody thought she had made a big mistake and would live to regret it, and I vowed and determined I was going to give her more than he could've given her. I was a good bricklayer, and I was especially good at arching and vaulting, and when a contractor or a boss mason had a cesspool to be built, he usually put me to work on it. We didn't have sewers down in this part of Staten Island, and still don't, and there were plenty of cesspools to be built. So, in 1899 I borrowed some money and went into business for myself, the business of building and cleaning cesspools. I made it my lifework. And I made good money, for around here. I built a good house for my wife, and I dressed her in the latest styles. I went up to New York once and bought her a dress for Easter that cost one hundred and six dollars; the six dollars was for alterations. And one Christmas I bought her a sealskin coat. And I bought pretty hats for her—velvet hats, straw hats, hats with feathers, hats with birds, hats with veils. And she appreciated everything I bought for her. 'Oh, George,' she'd say, 'you've gone too far this time. You've got to take it back.' 'Take it back, nothing!' I'd say. When Victrolas came out, I bought her the biggest one in the store. And I think I can safely say we set the best table in Sandy Ground. I lived in peace and harmony with her for thirty-two years, and they were the best years of my life. She died in

1928. Cancer. Two years later I married a widow named Mrs. Edith S. Cook. She died in 1938. They told me it was tumors, but it was cancer."

We came to a break in the privet hedge. Through the break I saw the white shapes of gravestones half-hidden in vines and scrub, and realized that we were at the entrance to the cemetery. "Here we are," said Mr. Hunter. He stopped, and leaned on the handle of the hoe, and continued to talk.

"I had one son by my first wife," he said. "We named him William Francis Hunter, and we called him Billy. When he grew up, Billy went into the business with me. I never urged him to, but he seemed to want to, it was his decision, and I remember how proud I was the first time I put it in the telephone book—George H. Hunter & Son. Billy did the best he could, I guess, but things never worked out right for him. He got married, but he lived apart from his wife, and he drank. When he first began to drink, I remembered my own troubles along that line, and I tried not to see it. I just looked the other way, and hoped and prayed he'd get hold of himself, but there came a time I couldn't look the other way any more. I asked him to stop, and I begged him to stop, and I did all I could, went to doctors for advice, tried this, tried that, but he wouldn't stop. It wasn't exactly he wouldn't stop, he couldn't stop. A few years ago, his stomach began to bother him. He thought he had an ulcer, and he started drinking more than ever—said whiskey dulled the pain. I finally got him to go to the hospital, and it wasn't any ulcer, it was cancer."

Mr. Hunter took a wallet from his hip pocket. It was a large, old-fashioned wallet, the kind that fastens with a strap slipped through a loop. He opened it and brought out a folded white silk ribbon.

"Billy died last summer," he continued. "After I had made the funeral arrangements, I went to the florist in Tottenville and ordered a floral wreath and picked out a nice wreath-ribbon to go on it. The florist knew me, and he knew Billy, and he made a very pretty wreath. The Sunday after Billy was buried, I walked over here to the cemetery to look at his grave, and the flowers on the wreath were all wilted and dead, but the ribbon was as pretty as ever, and I couldn't bear to let it lay out in the rain and rot, so I took it off and saved it." He unfolded the ribbon and held it up. Across it, in gold letters, were two words. "BELOVED SON," they said.

Mr. Hunter refolded the ribbon and returned it to his wallet. Then he put the hoe back on his shoulder, and we entered the cemetery. A little road went halfway into the cemetery, and a number of paths branched off from it, and both the road and the paths were hip-deep in broom sedge. Here and there in the sedge were patches of Queen Anne's lace and a weed that I didn't recognize. I pointed it out to Mr. Hunter.

"What is that weed in among the broom sedge and the Queen Anne's lace?" I asked.

"We call it red root around here," he said, "and what you call broom sedge we call beard grass, and what you call Queen Anne's lace we call wild carrot."

We started up the road, but Mr. Hunter almost immediately turned in to one of the paths and stopped in front of a tall marble gravestone, around which several kinds of vines and climbing plants were intertwined. I counted them, and there were exactly ten kinds—cat brier, trumpet creeper, wild hop, blackberry, morning glory, climbing false buckwheat, partridgeberry, fox grape, poison ivy, and one that I couldn't identify, nor could Mr. Hunter. "This is Uncle Daws Landin's grave," Mr. Hunter said. "I'm going to chop down some of this mess, so we can read the dates on his stone." He lifted the hoe high in the air and brought it down with great vigor, and I got out of his way. I went back into the road, and looked around me. The older graves were covered with trees and shrubs. Sassafras and honey locust and wild black cherry were the tallest, and they were predominant, and beneath them were chokeberry, bayberry, sumac, Hercules' club, spice bush, sheep laurel, hawthorn, and witch hazel. A scattering of the newer graves were fairly clean, but most of them were thickly covered with weeds and wild flowers and ferns. There were scores of kinds. The majority were the common kinds that grow in waste places and in dumps and in vacant lots and in old fields and beside roads and ditches and railroad tracks, and I could recognize them at a glance. Among these were milkweed, knotweed, ragweed, Jimson weed, pavement weed, catchfly, Jerusalem oak, bedstraw, goldenrod, cocklebur, butter-and-eggs, dandelion, bouncing Bet, mullein, partridge pea, beggar's-lice, sandspur, wild garlic, wild mustard, wild geranium, rabbit tobacco, old-field cinquefoil, bracken, New York fern, cinnamon fern, and lady fern. A good many of the others were unfamiliar to me, and I broke off the heads and upper branches of a number of these and stowed them in the pockets of my jacket, to look at later under a magnifying glass. Some of the graves had rusty iron-pipe fences around them. Many were unmarked, but were outlined with sea shells or bricks or round stones painted white or flowerpots turned upside down. Several had fieldstones at the head and foot. Several had wooden stakes at the head and foot. Several had Spanish bayonets growing on them. The Spanish bayonets were in full bloom, and little flocks of white moths were fluttering around their white, waxy, fleshy, bell-shaped, pendulous blossoms.

"Hey, there!" Mr. Hunter called out. "I've got it so we can see to read it now." I went back up the path, and we stood among the wrecked vines and looked at the inscription on the stone. It read:

DAWSON LANDIN

DEC. 18, 1828

FEB. 21, 1899

ASLEEP IN JESUS

"I remember him well," said Mr. Hunter. "He was a smart old man and a good old man—big and stout, very religious, passed the plate in church, chewed tobacco, took the New York *Herald,* wore a captain's cap, wore suspenders and a belt, had a peach orchard. I even remember the kind of peach he had in his orchard. It was a freestone peach, a late bearer, and the name of it was Stump the World."

We walked a few steps up the path, and came to a smaller gravestone. The inscription on it read:

SUSAN A. WALKER

MAR. 10, 1855

MAR. 25, 1912

A FAITHFUL FRIEND

"Born in March, died in March," said Mr. Hunter. "Fifty-seven years and fifteen days, as well as I can figure it out in my head. 'A Faithful Friend.' That hardly seems the proper thing to pick out and mention on a gravestone. Susan Walker was one of Uncle Daws Landin's daughters, and she was a good Christian woman. She did more for the church than any other woman in the history of Sandy Ground. Now, that's strange. I don't remember a thing about Uncle Daws Landin's funeral, and he must've had a big one, but I remember Susan Walker's funeral very well. There used to be a white man named Charlie Bogardus who ran a store at the corner of Woodrow Road and Bloomingdale Road, a general store, and he also had an icehouse, and he was also an undertaker. He was the undertaker for most of the country people around here, and he got some of the Rossville business and some of the Pleasant Plains business. He had a handsome old horse-drawn hearse. It had windows on both sides, so you could see the coffin, and it had silver fittings. Bogardus handled Susan Walker's funeral. I can still remember his two big black hearse-horses drawing the hearse up Bloomingdale Road, stepping just as slow, the way they were trained to do, and turning in to Crabtree Avenue, and proceeding on down to the cemetery. The horses had black plumes on their harnesses. Funerals were much sadder when they had horse-drawn hearses. Charlie Bogardus had a son named Charlie Junior, and Charlie Junior had a son named Willie, and when automobile hearses started coming in, Willie mounted the old hearse on an automobile chassis. It didn't look fish, fowl, or fox, but the Bogarduses kept on using it until they finally gave up the store and the icehouse and the undertaking business and moved away."

We left Susan Walker's grave and returned to the road and entered another path and stopped before one of the newer graves. The inscription on its stone read:

FREDERICK ROACH

1891–1955

REST IN PEACE

"Freddie Roach was a taxi-driver," Mr. Hunter said. "He drove a taxi in Pleasant Plains for many years. He was Mrs. Addie Roach's son, and she made her home with him. After he died, she moved in with one of her daughters. Mrs. Addie Roach is the oldest woman in Sandy Ground. She's the widow of Reverend Lewis Roach, who was an oysterman and a part-time preacher, and she's ninety-two years old. When I first came to Sandy Ground, she was still in her teens, and she was a nice, bright, pretty girl. I've known her all these years, and I think the world of her. Every now and then, I make her a lemon-meringue pie and take it to her, and sit with her awhile. There's a white man in Prince's Bay who's a year or so older than Mrs. Roach. He's ninety-three, and he'll soon be ninety-four. His name is Mr. George E. Sprague, and he comes from a prominent old South Shore family, and I believe he's the last of the old Prince's Bay oyster captains. I hadn't seen him for several years until just the other day I was over in Prince's, and I was going past his house on Amboy Road, and I saw him sitting on the porch. I went up and spoke to him, and we talked awhile, and when I was leaving he said, 'Is Mrs. Addie Roach still alive over in Sandy Ground?' 'She is,' I said. 'That is,' I said, 'she's alive as you or I.' 'Well,' he said, 'Mrs. Roach and I go way back. When she was a young woman, her mother used to wash for my mother, and she used to come along sometimes and help, and she was such a cheerful, pretty person my mother always said it made the day nicer when she came, and that was over seventy years ago.' 'That wasn't her mother that washed for your mother and she came along to help,' I said. 'That was her husband's mother. That was old Mrs. Matilda Roach.' 'Is that so?' said Mr. Sprague. 'I always thought it was her mother. Well,' he said, 'when you see her, tell her I asked for her.'"

We stepped back into the road, and walked slowly up it.

"Several men from Sandy Ground fought in the Civil War," Mr. Hunter said, "and one of them was Samuel Fish. That's his grave over there with the ant hill on it. He got a little pension. Down at the end of this row are some Bishop graves, Bishops and Mangins, and there's Purnells in the next row, and there's Henmans in those big plots over there. This is James McCoy's grave. He came from Norfolk, Virginia. He had six fingers on his right hand. Those graves over there all grown up in cockleburs are Jackson graves, Jacksons and Henrys and Landins. Most of the people lying in here were related to each other, some by blood, some by marriage, some close, some distant. If you started in at the gate and ran an imaginary line all the way through, showing who was related to who, the line would zigzag all over the cemetery. Do you see that row of big expensive stones standing up over there? They're all Cooleys. The Cooleys were free-Negro oystermen from Gloucester County, Virginia, and they came to Staten Island around the same time as the people from Snow Hill. They lived in Tottenville, but they belonged to the church in Sandy Ground. They were quite well-to-do. One of them, Joel Cooley, owned a forty-foot sloop. When the oyster beds were condemned, he retired on his savings and raised dahlias. He was a member of the Staten Island Horticultural Society, and his dahlias won medals at flower shows in Madison Square Garden. I've heard it said he was the first man on Staten Island to raise figs, and now there's fig bushes in back yards from one end of the island to the other. Joel Cooley had a brother named Obed Cooley who was very smart in school, and the Cooleys got together and sent him to college. They sent him to the University of Michigan, and he became a doctor. He practiced in Lexington, Kentucky, and he died in 1937, and he left a hundred thousand dollars. There used to be a lot of those old-fashioned names around here, Bible names. There was a Joel and an Obed and an Eben in the Cooley family, and there was an Ishmael and an Isaac and an Israel in the Purnell family. Speaking of names, come over here and look at this stone."

We stopped before a stone whose inscription read:

THOMAS WILLIAMS
AL MAJOR
1862–1928

"There used to be a rich old family down here named the Butlers," Mr. Hunter said. "They were old, old Staten Islanders, and they had a big estate over on the outside shore, between Prince's Bay and Tottenville, that they called Butler Manor. They even had a private race track. The last of the Butlers was Mr. Elmer T. Butler. Now, this fellow Thomas Williams was a Sandy Ground man who quit the oyster business and went to work for Mr. Elmer T. Butler. He worked for him many years, worked on the grounds, and Mr. Butler thought a lot of him. For some reason I never understood, Mr. Butler called him Al Major, a kind of nickname. And pretty soon everybody called him Al Major. In fact, as time went on and he got older, young people coming up took it for granted Al Major was his real name and called him Mr. Major. When he died, Mr. Butler buried him. And when he ordered the gravestone, he told the monument company to put both names on it, so there wouldn't be any confusion. Of course, in a few years he'll pass out of people's memory under both names—Thomas Williams, Al Major, it'll all be the same. To tell you the truth, I'm no great believer in gravestones. To a large extent, I think they come under the heading of what the old preacher called vanity—'vanity of vanities, all is vanity'—and by the old preacher I mean Ecclesiastes. There's stones in here that've only been up forty or fifty years, and you can't read a thing it says on them, and what difference does it make? God keeps His eye on those that are dead and buried the same as He does on those that are alive and walking. When the time comes the dead are raised, He won't need any directions where they're lying. Their bones may be turned to dust, and weeds may be growing out of their dust, but they aren't lost. He knows where they are; He knows the exact whereabouts of every speck of dust of every one of them. Stones rot the same as bones rot, and nothing endures but the spirit."

Mr. Hunter turned and looked back over the rows of graves.

"It's a small cemetery," he said, "and we've been

burying in it a long time, and it's getting crowded, and there's generations to come, and it worries me. Since I'm the chairman of the board of trustees, I'm in charge of selling graves in here, graves and plots, and I always try to encourage families to bury two to a grave. That's perfectly legal, and a good many cemeteries are doing it nowadays. All the law says, it specifies that the top of the box containing the coffin shall be at least three feet below the level of the ground. To speak plainly, you dig the grave eight feet down, instead of six feet down, and that leaves room to lay a second coffin on top of the first. Let's go to the end of this path, and I'll show you my plot."

Mr. Hunter's plot was in the last row, next to the woods. There were only a few weeds on it. It was the cleanest plot in the cemetery.

"My mother's buried in the first grave," he said. "I never put up a stone for her. My first wife's father, Jacob Finney, is buried in this one, and I didn't put up a stone for him, either. He didn't own a grave, so we buried him in our plot. My son Billy is buried in this grave. And this is my first wife's grave. I put up a stone for her."

The stone was small and plain, and the inscription on it read:

HUNTER

1877 CELIA 1928

"I should've had her full name put on it—Celia Ann," Mr. Hunter said. "She was a little woman, and she had a low voice. She had the prettiest little hands; she wore size five-and-a-half gloves. She was little, but you'd be surprised at the work she done. Now, my second wife is buried over here, and I put up a stone for her, too. And I had my name carved on it, along with hers."

This stone was the same size and shape as the other, and the inscription on it read:

HUNTER

1877 EDITH 1938

1869 GEORGE

"It was my plan to be buried in the same grave with my second wife," Mr. Hunter said. "When she died, I was sick in bed, and the doctor wouldn't let me get up, even to go to the funeral, and I couldn't attend to things the way I wanted to. At that time, we had a gravedigger here named John Henman. He was an old man, an old oysterman. He's dead now himself. I called John Henman to my bedside, and I specifically told him to dig the grave eight feet down. I told him I wanted to be buried in the same grave. 'Go eight feet down,' I said to him, 'and that'll leave room for me, when the time comes.' And he promised to do so. And when I got well, and was up and about again, I ordered this stone and had it put up. Below my wife's name and dates I had them put my name and my birth year. When it came time, all they'd have to put on it would be my death year, and everything would be in order. Well, one day about a year later I was talking to John Henman, and something told me he hadn't done what he had promised to do, so I had another man come over here and sound the grave with a metal rod, and just as I had suspected, John Henman had crossed me up; he had only gone six feet down. He was a contrary old man, and set in his ways, and he had done the way he wanted, not the way I wanted. He had always dug graves six feet down, and he couldn't change. That didn't please me at all. It outraged me. So, I've got my name on the stone on this grave, and it'll look like I'm buried in this grave."

He took two long steps, and stood on the next grave in the plot.

"Instead of which," he said, "I'll be buried over here in this grave."

He stooped down, and pulled up a weed. Then he stood up, and shook the dirt off the roots of the weed, and tossed it aside.

"Ah, well," he said, "it won't make any difference."

(1956)

Dragger Captain

The biggest fishing fleet in the vicinity of New York City is a fleet of thirty wooden draggers that works out of Stonington, Connecticut. Stonington is four local stops beyond New London on the New York, New Haven & Hartford. In the winter, when the trees are bare, a corner of its harbor can be glimpsed from a train. It covers a rocky jut in the mouth of Fishers Island Sound, it is close to fertile flounder grounds, it has two fish docks, and its harbor, protected by three riprap breakwaters, is an unusually safe one. Its population is approximately two thousand. There are elms on its sidewalks. On four of its narrow streets—Water, Main, Church, and Elm— are eight clapboard houses that were built in the eighteenth century. The gardens in back yards are fenced with discarded fish nets; some gardeners put seaweed under their tomatoes and skates and sculpin and other trash fishes under their rosebushes. It is an old port, once rich and busy, that has declined; from the Colonial period until the Civil War, it had shipyards, sail lofts, a ropewalk, a forge that made harpoons, a ship-biscuit bakery, and a whaling fleet, and it had a sealing fleet from around 1790 until around 1895. In the eighteen-seventies, this fleet brought in a hundred thousand sealskins a year for coats and lap robes. Nathaniel Brown Palmer, who discovered the Antarctic Continent, according to one school of geographers, and for whom Palmer Land in the Antarctic was named, and Edmund Fanning, who discovered the Fanning Islands in the Pacific, were Stonington sealing captains; they were looking for new seal rocks. Many of the draggermen are descendants of whalers and sealers. One Stonington sealer, Mr. Ben Chesebrough, is still around. There is a drafty shack adjacent to Johnny Bindloss's fish dock, at the foot of a lane off Water Street, in which the draggermen kill time when it is too rough or foggy to go out on the grounds. They sit on upended lobster traps and read the *Atlantic Fisherman* and drink coffee and play poker and sharpen knives and grumble. On such days, Mr. Ben sometimes drops in and talks about his experiences as a seal skinner long ago in the Antarctic. In the early summer, herds of seals would come up on the beaches of islands in the Antarctic to breed and while they were breeding the skinners would creep out from behind rocks and brain them by the dozens as cleanly as possible with clubs made of polished Connecticut oak; bullets would have marred the skins.

Stonington and Fulton Fish Market are closely linked. Several of the oldest commission firms in the market were founded by fishermen who came down from Stonington to handle shipments from relatives and friends and then branched out. Sam and Amos Chesebro (originally Chesebrough; they dropped the last three letters to save ink and time), who founded Chesebro Brothers, Robbins & Graham, were Stonington men. This firm occupies Stall 1 and is the biggest firm down there. Sam and Amos had long lives. Sam was approaching ninety when he died. Amos died a few years after him, in December, 1946, lacking a month of reaching ninety-three. He spent his last fifteen years reading and meditating and dozing in a sunny apartment on an upper floor of a house in Brooklyn Heights, directly across the East River from the market; on clear mornings he sat at a living-room window with a glass of whiskey and water at his elbow and, as if looking back through time at his youth, peacefully watched through binoculars the turmoil on the market piers. Others from Stonington or close by who came down and founded firms, or became partners in ones already founded, were Hiram Burnett, Frank Noyes, A. E. Potter,

George Moon, the Haley brothers, Caleb and Seabury, the Gates brothers, Stanton and Gurdon, and the
Keeney brothers, Frank, Gideon, and George. The
Stonington draggers catch twenty million pounds a
year for Fulton Market. They go out primarily for
flounders and they bring in five species—flukes,
blackbacks, yellowtails, witches, and windowpanes—
all of which differ in looks and flavor and all of which
dishonestly appear on menus under the catchall culi-
nary term "fillet of sole"; none of them belong to the
sole family. Another species, the Baptist flounder, is
caught in abundance but thrown back; it goes bad
shortly after it comes out of the water, whence its
name.

The Stonington draggers range from thirty to
seventy feet. They are built wide for their length and
about as close to the water as tugs. Half have gasoline
engines, and the other half, the newer ones, have
Diesels. Each has a cramped pilothouse. Each has a
combined cabin and galley containing from two to six
bunks, an oilcloth-covered table, two benches, and a
coal cookstove, on which there is always a big, sooty
pot of coffee. Each has a mast and a boom, from
which the towropes to the net depend. Each has a
winch for hoisting the loaded net aboard. Each has a
fish hold and an ice bin. The Stonington draggers are
well made and sturdy and are frequently overhauled.
Even so, lined up at the docks, with their seaweedy

nets hanging every which way from their booms to dry and with the harbor gulls fluttering down to snatch fish scraps off their decks, they always look gone to pot. They cost from ten to forty thousand dollars. A few are owned by absentees, but the majority are owned by their captains, or by their captains and crews, who are Portuguese, Italians, and old-stock Yankees. They fish off eastern Connecticut and western Rhode Island and on the coastal shelf south of Block Island in grounds known as the Mouth, the Yellow Bank, the Hell Hole, and the Mussel Bed, working chiefly in depths between sixty and a hundred and sixty feet. The crews prefer to stay on the grounds only one day at a time. They go out before dawn, weather permitting, and drag steadily all day, sorting and icing and barreling one haul while dragging for the next. They return at sundown and land their barrels, some at Bindloss's dock—once known as the Hancock dock, which dates back deep into sealing days—and the others at Tony Longo's dock, the old Steamboat Pier, which was used in times long past by the Stonington Line, whose side-wheel steamers ran daily between Stonington and New York. The barrels are loaded on trailer trucks owned by the proprietors of the docks and transported during the night to the stalls in Fulton Market. Occasionally, a dragger that has picked up an exceptionally heavy load does not go to its dock but makes an overnight run down Long Island Sound straight to the market. Stonington fish are among the freshest we get.

A dragger is a small trawler. The principal difference between the Stonington draggers and the trawlers that work out of Gloucester and Boston and New Bedford and stay on the Nova Scotian banks a week a trip is size. Trawlers are two and three times the size of draggers. Both use otter trawls, which are heavy, clumsy, wide-mouthed, cone-shaped nets that are slowly dragged over the bottom and take in all the fish in their paths. The otter trawl towed by a medium-sized Stonington dragger, a fifty-footer, is a hundred and ten feet long. The mouth is eighty feet wide but puckers up to half that width when fishing; it is kept open by two doors, or otter boards, which are about as big as house doors and are rigged at such an angle, one on each side, that the pressure of the water flares them out. Towing this net at two miles an hour, a dragger can strip the fish off ten acres of bottom in an hour. Otter trawls snag easily on obstructions, and a snagged trawl usually has to be abandoned. They are expensive; the smallest, even when rigged with homemade doors, costs a hundred dollars. A Stonington captain once snagged three in one morning; he went home and got in bed and stayed there until Sunday, when he showed up in church for the first time in years, exclaiming brokenly, as he walked up the aisle, "Pray for me! Pray for me!"

There are a great many shipwrecks, clumps of rocks, and other obstructions on the Stonington bottoms. The Hell Hole is the dirtiest. It is a ground of approximately six square miles in Block Island Sound, it is crisscrossed by coastwise shipping lanes, and there are two dozen wrecks lying in it, some of which always have rotting otter trawls hanging on them. Every now and then, after a gale or a hurricane has opened up a wreck and washed it out, a haul made in the Hell Hole is dumped on the deck of a dragger, and human bones—most often a skull or a pelvic bone; they seem to last the longest in salt water—are found among the fish. On the bottom of the Mussel Bed, a ground in the open ocean off Block Island, there is a group of immense beds of horse mussels, the lips of whose shells point upward and are jagged and sharp. Dragger captains must know the locations of these beds and keep acquainted with their endlessly changing contours, and they must take great pains to skirt them; a net that even grazes one will come up with scores of holes cut and chafed in its underside, through which the fish have escaped. This ground also contains some wrecks. One is a collier, the *Black Point,* which was torpedoed by a German submarine in May, 1945, in the last week of the European war. The submarine lies nearby; it was depth-bombed by a destroyer as it tried to get away. The Yellow Bank is a narrow ground that runs along the Rhode Island coast from the lighthouse at Watch Hill to Weekapaug Point, a distance of six miles, and its bottom is broken here and there by beds of sponges—elephant flop sponge, which grows in slippery yellow lumps the size of cabbages, and a limp, tentacular species called dead man's fingers. Both of them are worthless. These animals do not damage nets, but they clog them, and they have to be sorted out of hauls, one by one, and thrown back, a time-wasting task. Some time ago, a net that had been dragged into a sponge bed came up bearing two and a half barrels of fish messily mixed in among approximately fifteen barrels of sponges. In the Mouth, a ground at the mouth of the Thames River, below New London, there are rank patches of seaweed, predominantly bladder wrack, the black, bulby kind on which live lobsters are displayed in the windows of seafood restaurants, and these have to be dodged for the same reason. All these grounds except the Mouth were entered a number of times during the war by enemy submarines, and Army and Navy aircraft dropped hundreds of aerial depth bombs in them, particularly in the Mussel Bed. Some of the heavier bombs, mostly six-hundred-and-fifty-pounders, stuck in the mud and did not explode, and are lying there still. They will be a menace for years, like the German mines in French farm land. There are suspect areas in the Hell Hole and the Mussel Bed that are shunned by draggermen and spoken of as the bomb beds. In the old days, when a winch creaked and backfired as it began to hoist a net off the bottom, indicating an exceptionally heavy haul, crews were elated and someone always shouted, "Money in the bank!," but nowadays the noise of a straining winch makes them uneasy; the net might be heavy with flounders or it might have a bomb in it. Five draggers—the *Carl F.,* the *George A. Arthur,* the *Gertrude,* the *Marise,* and the *Nathaniel B. Palmer*— have brought up bombs in their nets. The first four had their nets on deck before the bombs in them, hidden by fish, were discovered. Rather than attempt to dump them back, each went cautiously to the nearest dock, to which Navy bomb-disposal officers were summoned. The bomb caught by the fifth dragger, the *Palmer,* was plainly visible, but it exploded shortly after the net hove out of the water, while the crew stood staring at it, wondering what to do. It blasted the dragger and three of the four men in the crew to pieces; the fourth man was freakishly thrown clear.

Because of these hazards—rocks, wrecks, mussel beds, sponge beds, bladder wrack, and bombs—it is necessary for a dragger captain to have a picture in his mind of what lies beneath every possible foot of water in the grounds he works. A captain's standing among his colleagues and the amount of ice and oil he can get on credit from the dock proprietor are based on his knowledge of the bottoms and his thriftiness with gear, and not on the quantity of fish he catches. A raw captain may drag blindly and bring up huge hauls for a while, but sooner or later he will snag or mussel-cut so many nets that his overhead will eat up his profits. The most highly respected captain in the Stonington fleet is a sad-eyed, easy-going Connecticut Yankee named Ellery Franklin Thompson, a member of a family that has fished and clammed and crabbed and attended to lobster traps in these waters for three hundred years.

Ellery—he says he is called Captain Thompson or Mr. Thompson only by people who want to get something out of him—is captain and owner of the gasoline dragger *Eleanor,* which usually carries a crew of three, including himself. Ellery is forty-seven years old and has been a draggerman for thirty years. He has worked out of five Connecticut ports—New London, Groton, Noank, Mystic, and Stonington, all of which are close together—and out of two Rhode Island ports, Newport and Point Judith. Stonington has been his home port since 1930. He keeps the *Eleanor* at Bindloss's dock, but he lives in New

London, fourteen miles away, and drives an automobile to and fro. He lives in a four-gabled, shingle-sided, two-story house on Crystal Avenue. His widowed mother, Mrs. Florence Thompson, keeps house for him. He used to sleep in a woven-wire bunk aboard the *Eleanor* and do his own cooking year in and year out, going home only for Sundays, but in recent years, because of rheumatism, he has got so he rests better in a bed. He says he has discovered that home life has one disadvantage. He is a self-taught B-flat-trumpet player. While living on the *Eleanor,* he spent many evenings in the cabin by himself practicing hymns and patriotic music. Sometimes, out on the grounds, if he had a few minutes to kill, he would go below and practice. One afternoon, blundering around the Hell Hole in a thick summer fog, he grew tired of cranking the foghorn and got out his trumpet and stood on deck and played "The Star-Spangled Banner" over and over, alarming the crews of other draggers fogbound in the area, who thought an excursion boat was bearing down on them. After he went back to sleeping at home, he continued to practice in the evenings, but he had to give it up before long because of its effect on his mother's health. "At that time," he says, "I was working hard on three hymns—'Up from the Grave He Arose,' 'There Is a Fountain Filled with Blood,' and 'What a Friend We Have in Jesus.' I had 'What a Friend' just about where

I wanted it. One evening after supper, I went in the parlor as usual and Ma was sitting on the settee reading the *Ladies' Home Journal* and I took the easy chair and went to work on 'What a Friend.' I was running through it the second or third time when, all of a sudden, Ma bust out crying. I laid my trumpet down and I asked her what in the world was the matter. 'That trumpet's what's the matter,' Ma said. 'It makes me sad.' She said it made her so sad she was having nightmares and losing weight. Under the circumstances, I decided whatever trumpet practice I did in the future, I would do it four or five miles out at sea."

Ellery is five feet nine. He is thin and rather frail. Aboard the *Eleanor,* he wears knee boots, trousers that are leathery with fish blood and slime, a heavy plaid woolen shirt, a pea jacket, and a misshapen old flop-brim hat that always has some toothpicks and pencil stubs stuck in its band. He walks with a pronounced stoop, favoring his left shoulder, where the rheumatism has settled, and he takes his time. "If I start to hustle and bustle," he says, "everything I eat repeats and repeats." He abhors hurry; he thinks that humanity in general has got ahead of itself. He once threatened to fire a man in his crew because he worked too hard. Ellery's face is narrow and bony and, except for the sadness in his deep-set eyes, impassive. His ears stick out, he is long-nosed, and he has a mustache. His voice is nasal but pleasant, and his Adam's apple works when he talks. A woman in Stonington in her nineties, a town character, once told him that he had an old-fashioned face. "Men's faces nowadays are either empty or worried to death, like they're dreading something," she said. "You look the way the old Yankees around here looked when I was a girl."

"Don't fool yourself," Ellery said. "I guess I'm dreading something, too."

"What are you dreading, Ellery?" she asked.

Ellery shrugged his shoulders. "I don't know," he said. "I wish to God I did know."

Ellery is companionable but reserved. He often sits out a weathery day in the dock shack with other draggermen, listening with enjoyment to the trade gossip and the story-telling but saying little himself. When he does get into a talking mood, much of what he says is ironical. He is deeply skeptical. He once said that the older he gets the more he is inclined to believe that humanity is helpless. "I read the junk in the papers," he said, "and sometimes, like I'm eating in some eating joint and I can't help myself, I listen to the junk on the radio, and the way it looks to me, it's blind leading blind out of the frying pan into the fire, world without end. It's like me and Doc Clendening. There used to be a department in the New London *Day* called 'Diet and Health.' It was run by Dr. Logan

Clendening, and he was always bright and cheerful. 'Keep smiling!' he'd say. 'Worry will kill you. A good hearty laugh,' he'd say, 'is the best medicine. If you've got high blood pressure, laugh! If you've got low blood pressure, laugh! The more you laugh, the longer you'll live.' When I was down in the dumps, I always enjoyed 'Diet and Health.' It was the first thing I'd turn to. It cheered me up. And then one day I picked up the paper and it said that 'Diet and Health' wouldn't appear no more because Dr. Clendening had cut his throat."

Two things are mainly responsible for Ellery's outlook: rheumatism and the depression. He is one of those who are unable to forget the depression. Fish prices were at rock bottom in the thirties, and draggermen had to take foolish risks and double and triple their production to barely get by. Ellery had one brother, Morris, six years younger, who was also a dragger captain. While working in a December gale off Newport in 1931, Morris was knocked senseless by a huge wave that broke on the deck of his dragger; the wave, receding, sucked him in, and he drowned. "He shouldn't have been out there," Ellery says, "but the poor boy had just started a family and prices were dropping and he was fighting hard to make a living." Ellery and his father and several friends of the family took the *Eleanor* out while the gale was still in progress and began to drag for Morris's body. On the morning of the third day, when they had almost decided to quit and go in, it came up in the net.

Ellery is about as self-sufficient as a man can be. He has no wife, no politics, and no religion. "I put off getting married until I got me a good big boat," he says. "When I got the boat and got it paid for, the depression struck. There's mighty few women that'll eat fish three times a day, and that's about all I had to offer. I kept putting it off until times got better. When times got better, I got the rheumatism. And a man in his middle forties with the chronic rheumatism, there's not much of the old Romeo left in him." Ellery is a member of only one organization. "I'm a Mason," he says. "Aside from that, the only thing I belong to is the human race." His father was a Republican and his mother is a Democrat; he says he has never put any dependence in either party and has never once voted for anybody. His family belongs to the Baptist Church; he says he has managed somehow to get along without it. "I enjoy hymns," he says. "I enjoy the old ones, the gloomy ones. I used to go to church just to hear the good old hymns, but the sermons finally drove me away."

Ellery's ancestors on both sides—his mother was a Chapman—came from England in the sixteen-thirties and settled near the mouth of the Connecticut River, probably in the Saybrook Colony. Both families have stuck pretty close to the coast of eastern Connecticut, and the majority of the men have been fishermen, mariners, or shipwrights. Some were whalers and sealers. "I'm widely related," Ellery says, "but damn the benefit in that." Ellery was born in Mystic, which is five miles from Stonington. When he was around ten, the family moved to New London. He is one of four children, two of whom, Morris and an elder sister, Louise, are dead. Eleanor, a younger sister, is the wife of a switchman on the New Haven; the dragger *Eleanor* was named for her. Ellery's father, Frank Thompson, who died in 1936, was a fisherman, but he occasionally did other kinds of work. One year he was a quartermaster on a famous old Long Island Sound passenger steamer, the *City of Worcester;* another year he was a mate on an ocean-going tug, the Thames Tow Boat Company's *Minnie,* that towed coal barges from Norfolk, Virginia, to New London; during the Spanish-American War he was master of a patrol boat, the *Gypsy,* that guided ships through mine fields off the harbor of New London; and for a while he ran a ferry on the Thames, between Groton and New London; but he spent most of his life hand-lining and dragging in the Mouth. He was one of the first American fishermen to use the otter trawl, which is a British net. "Pa was a restless man, but a good man, a good provider," Ellery says. "He had one bad habit. He played the trombone. He could do nearly about as much damage with a trombone as I can with a trumpet."

Ellery's father kept his dragger, the *Florence,* a thirty-one-footer, which was named for Mrs. Thompson, at the Old Fish Dock in New London. "I spent the happiest days of my life on that dock," Ellery says. "It was a perfect place for a boy. It was right across the tracks from the New Haven station. If you got tired looking at boats, you could step over to the station and watch a freight highball through like a bat out of hell for Boston. I despised school. I don't mean I didn't like it. Oh, Jesus, I despised it. Whatever I learned in school, I learned a whole lot more down on the Old Fish Dock. Like Pa would drop a barrel in the water off the end of the dock and teach me how to harpoon a swordfish without getting my tail wound up in the line; the barrel would be the swordfish. Or some other man would teach me how to stick little wooden plugs in the hinges of lobsters' claws; that locks their claws, so they can't kill each other during shipment. I learned how to scale and gut, how to mend nets, how to read charts, how to cut a fishhook out of your hand, how to crate crabs, and how to tie all kinds of knots and bends and hitches and splices. There were some old, old fishermen on that dock. Some went down in the whale with Jonah, to hear them tell it. They didn't go out much any more. They mostly just sat around, hawking and spitting and God-damning everything in sight. They were full of old, handed-down secrets and sayings. I learned two things from them. I learned how to judge weather, and I learned how to take the good Lord's name in vain. Like all fish docks, this dock had a shack on it with a kerosene stove inside, and I learned how to make coffee. That's important. There's nobody so worthless as a fisherman who can't make a good, strong pot of coffee. In the summer, the Block Island steamer used one side of the fish dock. It met three trains a day. Back then, Block Island was a resort for the rich. If you weren't quite rich enough for Newport, you went to one of those big wooden hotels on Block Island. It was great fun to watch the people get on and off the steamer. Some days, like the Fourth, they'd have a band aboard. The first drunk woman I ever saw was an old sister they took off the Block Island steamer. She was white-haired, and she was so saturated she didn't know Jack from jump rope. Somebody's mother. It was a revelation to me. Around that time—I must've been eleven or twelve—there was a Greek café near the station and up above were rooms for rent, and sometimes I'd notice a woman sitting in the window of one of the rooms for rent; she'd crook a finger at some man passing below or give him a wink. I'd try my damnedest to figure that out. The facts of life. If the boats were out on the grounds and nothing doing on the dock, I'd sit in the shack and read Frank books. Oh, Jesus, I enjoyed Frank books. They were called the Gun Boat Series. There was 'Frank on a Gun Boat,' 'Frank Before Vicksburg,' 'Frank on the Lower Mississippi,' 'Frank in the Woods,' and 'Frank the Young Naturalist.' I've still got some Frank books on my dresser at home. Every so often, I get one down. You take 'Frank on the Lower Mississippi'—I bet I've read it thirty times. When I was sixteen, I got into first-year high school, but I couldn't stand it. I went to Pa and I told him, 'One more day of that mess— *amo, amas, amat*—just one more day, and I'll drown myself.' Pa said he guessed he'd sooner have an ignorant living son than a highly educated dead one, and next morning I went out on the grounds with him."

In 1920, after fishing with his father for several years, Ellery borrowed four thousand dollars from a firm of fish shippers in New London and bought a dragger of his own, the *Grace and Lucy.* He lived on flounders and coffee, cut corners, went out in foul and fair, and paid for her in a year and ten months. He had a lot of affection for her, but she was top-heavy and she rolled and pounded. In 1924, he sold her and bought another, which he named the *Louise,* after his sister. "The *Louise* was rolly, too," he says. "She was the *Grace and Lucy* all over again." These were small draggers; both were less than forty feet. At the end of 1926, Ellery decided to build a new one, a bigger one. "I didn't want a whore's dream," he says. "On the other hand, I didn't want a barge. I wanted a good, plain working boat that would squat down in the water and let the net know who was boss. I wanted to crowd everything I could up forward, engine and winch and cabin and pilothouse and life dory, so I'd have plenty of deck in the stern to empty my net on. I tried to explain this to some boatyard fellows, some professional designers, but they had ideas of their own. They tried to talk me into one of those boats with so much labor-saving gear on them you're so busy saving labor you can't get any work done. I decided I'd take a chance and design my own boat, about like a fellow up for some awful crime would decide to be his own lawyer." Ellery made a study of several draggers in the Noank and Stonington fleets whose behavior in rough water he admired, and he went to the boatyards and examined the designs from which they had been built. Then he sat down with some dime-store calipers and rulers and made inboard and deck-arrangement plans for a fifty-foot dragger to be called the *Eleanor.* He made them on the backs of two wrinkled Coast and Geodetic charts. He showed these plans to a friend named Ernest C. Daboll. Mr. Daboll was, as he still is, editor of the *New England Almanac and Farmer's Friend,* familiarly called "Daboll's Weather Book," which has been published in New London by the Daboll family almost continuously since 1772. Many old fishermen still have more respect for its weather predictions than for those broadcast on the radio. Mr. Daboll is also a surveyor and draftsman. He corrected Ellery's plans and had them blueprinted. Early in 1927, Ellery sold the *Louise,* withdrew his savings, borrowed some more money, and took these blueprints to the Rancocas boatyard, in Delanco, New Jersey, down near Camden. "The *Eleanor* was launched the middle of May," Ellery says. "Oh, Jesus, I was nervous. When I started up the coast with her, I took a quart of gin along, in case of disappointment, but I didn't even unscrew the cap. Much to my satisfaction, she turned out good. In fact, she turned out perfect." Ellery is disinclined to tell how much the *Eleanor* cost. "What she cost doesn't mean a thing," he says. "She's getting old and frazzly, but I wouldn't sell her for what she cost, or nowheres near. I wouldn't sell her for fifteen thousand dollars."

In his first two boats, Ellery was nomadic. If a rumor came down from Martha's Vineyard that there was a phenomenal run of cod off Gay Head, he would fill his gasoline tanks and go up there. If he heard that swordfish had been sighted foraging on mackerel off Montauk Point, he would sharpen some lily irons and go out and try to strike a few. One morning, in the *Louise,* working out of New London, he and his mate went on a scallop-dredging trip, fully intending to be back that night. Instead, for three weeks they strayed down the coast, dredging until nightfall and then putting in at the nearest port to express their scallops to Fulton Market. They reached Sheepshead Bay before turning back. "If there was a speakeasy near the fish dock in those ports, and there usually was," Ellery says, "we'd hole up in it and hobnob with the riffraff. I remember one speakeasy down on Great South Bay that was run by three sisters. All were red-headed and all were widows. They were called the Three Merry Widows. It was a disgraceful way of life, and I sure did enjoy it." Ellery found that the *Eleanor* was much more of a responsibility than his other boats. Shortly after getting her, he quit wandering and began concentrating on the Mouth, the Yellow Bank, and the Hell Hole.

There are two kinds of dragger captains: those who go out every day the weather allows and drag all over everywhere, figuring if they cover enough bottom they are bound to run into fish sooner or later, and those who carefully pick their days and drag only in areas where they are pretty sure fish are congregating. In his youth, Ellery was of the first kind; he is now the best example in the Stonington fleet of the second kind. He has a vast memory of the way the six species of flounders inhabiting the Stonington grounds have behaved in all seasons under all sorts of weather conditions. Consequently, he can foretell their migrations, sometimes to the day. Blackbacks, for example, the sweetest-meated of the flounders, spend the summer in the cold water offshore. Some time in the late fall, they begin moving inshore by the millions to the shallows, where they spawn. The biggest hauls are made during this migration. Ellery is always ready for the blackbacks. He knows the routes they follow and the best places to intercept them. Frank Muise, his mate, and Charlie Brayman, his third man, profess to believe that he thinks like a flounder. "Ellery doesn't need much sleep," Brayman says. "He only sleeps four or five hours. The rest of the night, he lies in bed and imagines he's a big bull flounder out on the ocean floor. When the black-backs get restless, he gets restless. One morning he shows up at the dock with an odd look in his eye and he says, 'The blackbacks commenced moving into the coves last night.' And I say, 'How the hell do you know?' And he says, 'Let's go out to the Hell Hole and try the fifteen-fathom curve off the Nebraska Shoal.' Or he says, 'Let's go up to the Mouth and drag in between Bartlett Reef and the North Dumpling.' He never misses. We go where he says and we always hit them where they're good and thick." Ellery has a simpler explanation. "I take a look at the weather," he says, "and I act accordingly."

Ellery is also an extraordinarily skillful wreck fisher. Fish forgather in great numbers around wrecks, some to feed on the mollusks, crustaceans, sea worms, and other organisms that they harbor, and some to feed on those that are feeding on these organisms. If pickings elsewhere are thin, a few of the more self-confident captains will risk their nets to get at such fish. By trial and error and by hearsay, Ellery long ago learned the location and shape and condition—whether sitting, lying on a side, or broken up—of every wreck in the Mouth and the Hell Hole. On calm, clear days, when he can take accurate ranges on rocks and buoys and on landmarks ashore, he goes out and methodically drags up close to a dozen or so of these. The others are so decayed and their pieces scattered about so treacherously that even he will not approach them. He usually starts with the *Larchmont,* a Providence–to–New York side-wheel passenger steamer that collided with the three-masted schooner *Harry Knowlton* during a snowstorm on the night of February 11, 1907, drowning over a hundred and thirty people, and ends with a coal barge that sank from a leak in May, 1944. He drags around the barge more for the coal that spills out of it during storms than for fish. He burns this coal in the *Eleanor*'s galley stove. Some nights, he fills the back seat of his automobile with Hell Hole coal and takes it home.

Ellery is an almost overly cautious captain, and he says that wreck fishing made him so. "Once I heard a contractor tell about cutting a ditch through a grave-yard," he says. "It reminded me of wreck fishing. I've brought up bones in my net many and many a time, and I've brought up skulls or parts of skulls several times. Oh, Jesus! Once I brought up a jawbone with nine teeth left in it, and there was a gold filling in every tooth; some had middle fillings and side fill-ings. Whoever he was—him or her, I couldn't tell which—the poor soul sure God wasted a lot of time in the dentist chair. Once I was fishing with my brother Morris. I was below eating lunch and Morris was on deck sorting a haul and he found a skull in a bunch of seaweed. The roots of the seaweed had grown around the skull and had kept it intact—the lower jaw was still attached to it, and you could open and shut the jaws with your hands. Morris was stand-ing there, looking at the skull and opening and shut-ting the jaws, when I came on deck munching on a big juicy peach. Morris looked at me, and then he looked at that toothy jaw, and then he took sick.

"All kinds of odds and ends come up in the net. One day a bucket of U.S. Navy paint came up, a five-gallon bucket of battleship gray. We prized the lid off and there wasn't a thing wrong with it I could see. Some sailor probably took a sudden dislike to it and heaved it in. We used it on the *Eleanor*. Another day, what came up only a woman's pink lace shimmy. Some woman on a summer yacht probably got a couple of whiskey sours in her and flung it off. Oh, it was a pretty thing. It had roses and butterflies on it. We tied it to a stay and flew it like a flag all that summer. Johnny Bindloss said no doubt some mermaid off Newport lost it. 'Over around Newport,' he said, 'even the mermaids wear pink lace shimmies.' Back during prohibition, there were some rum runners around eastern Connecticut. Some were Canucks and some were local boys. They used to buoy their booze in shoal water in the Hell Hole. They'd wrap the bottles in straw and sew them up in waterproof tarpaulin bags, twenty-four bottles to a bag. They were called buoy bags. Sometimes a storm'd part one from the buoy and it'd go wandering around on the bottom. One hot August afternoon, we emptied the net and out dropped a buoy bag. Twenty-four bottles of square-bottle Scotch. The crew wanted to pitch right in, but I could just visualize the consequences, so I argued and pleaded we ought to store it and use it in the winter for chills. So we stored it. Fifteen minutes later, the mate complained he had a chill. Then the third man's teeth began to chatter. Then I began to feel a little shivery myself. It was a week before things got back to normal. I don't mind buoy bags. It's the bones I mind. I had a mate once, a peculiar man, a Rhode Islander, and every time a bone came up, or anything else unusual, he'd squat down and study it. 'Throw that thing back where it came from,' I'd tell him. He'd study it some more, and he'd say, 'Ellery, there's many and many a secret buried out there in that Hell Hole.' And I'd say, 'Damn the secrets! Please do like I told you and throw that thing overboard.' Oh, I dread those bones. There but for the grace of God go I. Sometimes I take chances. Like a fog comes up, and I keep right on dragging. Then, all of a sudden, I think of those bones, and I don't fool around no more; I open her up and I head for the dock."

Although Ellery puts in an appearance at Bindloss's dock every weekday, usually before dawn, he seldom goes out on the grounds more than three days a week. Last year, he went out only a hundred and thirty days. Nevertheless, he shipped seventeen hundred and twenty-six barrels to Fulton Market, each holding approximately two hundred pounds of fish. There are boats that went out one-third again as many days and did not catch as much. Ellery ships to John Feeney, Inc., in Stall 13. Feeney's is the company that once employed Alfred E. Smith as a basket boy. Ellery is not the kind of man who will talk about how much he makes. "That's what's known as nobody's business," he says. On a fish dock, everybody knows everybody else's business, and three of Ellery's closest friends estimate he cleared six thousand dollars last year, maybe a thousand more, maybe a thousand less. His mate and his third man probably cleared between twenty-five hundred and three thousand each. Like all captain-owners in the Stonington fleet, Ellery works on shares with his crew under the forty-per-cent system; that is, at the end of each week, from the *Eleanor*'s earnings, less operating expenses (gasoline, oil, ice, and barrels), forty per cent is subtracted. This percentage, called the boat's share, goes to Ellery; out of it, he pays for nets and gear, repairs, drydocking, insurance, taxes, and so on. The balance is split equally among Ellery, Muise, and Brayman.

Young draggermen regard Ellery with awe because of his frugality with gear. He once went a year and seven months without snagging a net. Unlike most draggermen, he doesn't buy ready-made nets; he buys netting by the yard and makes his own. He gets the netting from George Wilcox, who runs a net loft on his farm in Quiambaug Cove, a crossroads village between Stonington and Mystic. There is a sign in this loft which reads, "NO CREDIT EXTENDED IN HERE UNLESS OVER 75 YRS OF AGE & ACCOM-PANIED BY GRANDPARENTS." "I'm related to George," Ellery says. "I guess we're cousins. My grandmother on Pa's side was a Wilcox. They're a long-lived set of people. George is in his eighties and the Wilcoxes don't hardly consider him full-grown;

he's got two brothers and a sister older than him. There was another brother, but he died some months ago. His name was Jess. Jess was ninety-three years old and getting on close to ninety-four, but he was still able to do a little light work around the farm. A few days before he died, he was breaking up some boulders with a sledge hammer, so he could use them in a stone fence. He had a blood blister on his left thumb he'd got shingling a roof and couldn't use his left hand at all and he was swinging the sledge hammer with one arm and the boulders were great big ones and the job was taking him twice as long as it ordinarily would and it aggravated him. A pouring-down rain came up and he wouldn't stop. He worked right through it and he got the pneumonia. The only reason he died, they took him to the hospital. Jess never slept good in a strange bed. Around midnight, he got up in the dark and put on his clothes, intending to slip downstairs and strike out for home, but he fell over something and broke his hip. The Wilcoxes used to operate a big fish-scrap factory on the Cove, the Wilcox Fertilizer Company. That's the reason they're so long-lived. The factory was just across the yard from the house and the prevailing wind blew the fish-scrap smell right into the house. This smell was so strong it killed all the germs in the air, and it was so rich it nourished you and preserved you. People in poor health for miles around learned about this and used to come in droves and sit all day on the porch, especially people with the asthma and the dropsy. Some days, there'd be so many sitting on the porch, getting the benefit of the smell, that it was quite a struggle for the Wilcoxes to get in and out of the house."

Ellery is the most skillful and the most respected of the captains in the Stonington fleet, and he is also the least ambitious. His knowledge of the behavior of flounders is so acute that he could double his production without straining himself, but he doesn't see any point in doing so. There are four reasons for this. First, he has rheumatism. Second, he is a self-taught oil painter. He prefers to paint when it is too stormy or foggy to drag, but if a painting looks as if it might turn out good, he will stay with it for days on end of perfect fishing weather. Third, he is an amateur oceanographer, a kind of unofficial member of the staff of the Bingham Oceanographic Laboratory at Yale University, and this takes up quite a lot of his time. Fourth, he lacks an itch for money. He makes a good living and considers that sufficient. He says he owns a boat, an automobile, a house and lot, seventy-five books, a trumpet, a straight razor, and a Sunday suit, and can't think of anything else he particularly wants.

The way Ellery disposes of the lobsters he picks

up in his net exemplifies his attitude toward money. There are lobsters in all the grounds dragged by the Stonington fleet. They are thickest in the Hell Hole, where swarms of them live in, under, and around the old shipwrecks that lie there. In the summer and fall, a few are caught in every drag. Now and then, a couple of bushels come up in a single haul, in among the fish. They bring high prices. The majority wind up in New York seafood restaurants as choice Maine lobsters; in these restaurants all lobsters, even those from Sheepshead Bay, come from Maine. All the captains except Ellery ship the young, combative, bronzy blue-green ones to Fulton Market and keep the culls and jumbos for their own tables. (The culls are those that have recently molted and whose new shells have not yet hardened, and those with one or both claws snapped off in fights or while mating. The jumbos are the sluggish, barnacle-incrusted, stringy-meated giants—old ones, who can be captured only in nets, since they have grown too big to go through the mouths of traps; the record for the fleet is a cock lobster that weighted twenty-two pounds and was fit only for salads and Newburgs.) Ellery does just the opposite. He selects the finest he catches and sets them aside for himself and his crew and ships the rest. "Let the rich eat the culls," he says. The third man in a three-handed fishing crew is supposed to do the cooking, but Ellery attends to most of it on the

Eleanor; he is one of those who believe that to get a thing done right you have to do it yourself. He is a matchless lobster chef. He boils and he broils and he makes lobster chowder, but most often he boils. He puts a tub of fresh sea water on the little coal stove in the cabin and heats it until it spits. He wraps his lobsters in seaweed and drops them in, half a dozen in a batch, and times them with a rusty alarm clock that hangs from a cup hook on the underside of a shelf above the stove; after exactly fifteen minutes, he dips them out. He lets them cool slowly, so that the meat won't shrink and become flavorless and rubbery, the common condition of cold boiled lobsters in restaurants, and then he heaps them on the cracked ice in the ice bin in the forward fish hold. He and his crew—Frank, the mate, and Charlie, the third man—reach in and get a lobster any time they feel like it. They eat them standing on deck. They smack them against the rail to crack the shells, pluck out the tail and claw meat, and chuck the rest overboard. One fall day, out on the Hell Hole, the three of them ate fourteen in between meals.

Ellery began to paint in the winter of 1930. At that time, he was sleeping aboard the *Eleanor,* at Bindloss's dock in Stonington, going home to New London to see his mother only on Sundays. In school, in her teens, Mrs. Thompson went to an art class, and several prim paintings of flowers she did still hang in her parlor. That winter, because she complained about being by herself so much, Ellery tried to reawaken this interest. In Brater's, a small art-supplies store in New London, he bought some stretched canvases and a set of paints and brushes. "Ma tried, but she couldn't somehow seem to pick up where she'd left off," Ellery says. "Her hands were too stiff. I had all that art gear laying around, and one Sunday afternoon I took a notion I'd paint me a picture. Ma gave me some directions and told me to start out with a rose, but I started out with the *Titanic* hitting the iceberg. I worked on it four Sundays. I didn't have much trouble with the *Titanic* or the iceberg, but the poor souls bobbing around in the water like to drove me crazy." He called the painting "Nearer My God to Thee." His mother admired it; she had it framed and hung it in the parlor between two of hers and called the neighbors in. "To tell the truth," Ellery says, "that made me proud." He took the art gear to Stonington and began to spend off hours scrutinizing objects around the dock, getting the look of them in his head, and then doing paintings of them—a battered tin bucket, a clam rake, a scallop dredge with fragments of scallop shells sticking to it, a capstan, an anchor. A lobster buoy is a block of wood, most often two feet long, which is attached by a tarred rope to a lobster trap and which floats above it, marking its position. Buoys are painstakingly and sometimes beautifully whittled into a variety of shapes and are brightly painted, usually in stripes in three colors; each lobsterman has a different set of colors; like racing silks, they denote ownership. Some discarded and barnacle-speckled buoys heaped any old way on the dock caught Ellery's eye and he did a painting of them. He did three paintings of animals—two fish-house cats hatefully eying each other at the mouth of an overturned bait barrel, a cormorant of a kind known locally as the black shag roosting on a mooring stake, a herd of rats scampering single file along the ridge of a breakwater in the moonlight. The breakwater rats are notorious around Stonington, and Ellery did a series of pencil sketches as well as the painting of them. They are wharf rats that migrated to the outer breakwater in Stonington harbor, where they nest in the riprap and grow enormous on dead fish washed up by the tide. Some draggermen keep a supply of rocks and brickbats aboard and, passing the breakwater on their way to and from the grounds, amuse themselves by harassing the rats. Presently, Ellery began using the *Eleanor* as his subject. He painted her in rough water with her net down, and he painted her with a haul of flounders dumped on her deck and a flock of gulls hovering above, and he painted her at Bindloss's dock with her net drying in the wind and a red sun going down behind her. He worked meticulously, putting in every detail he could find room for. One of the pilothouse windows has a zigzag crack across it; he always put this crack in, with the identical zigs and zags. "I like to show everything," he says. "If I had my way, I'd show the nailheads in the planks and the knots in the ropes and the stitches in the flag, but Ma thinks that makes a picture look tacky." In about a year, he did sixteen paintings of the *Eleanor*.

One Sunday morning in August, 1931, Ellery put his most recent paintings in his automobile to take home and show his mother. He stopped at a filling station near Groton on U.S. 1A for a tank of gas, and the proprietor, an old acquaintance, saw them on the back seat and looked them over and asked if he could put one in his window. " 'Why, hell yes,' I told him," Ellery says. "He picked one out, the biggest, and he figured there ought to be a price on it, make it look professional, so we cracked some jokes about that, and finally he stuck a sticker on it reading one hundred dollars. He laughed and I laughed. It wasn't more than an hour and a half later he phoned me there was a party down there wanted to buy it, a man from New York who was building a summer home at Groton Long Point. He was planning a marine room and wanted some boat pictures for it. He took my address and drove to the house—he surprised me; didn't look odd at all—and inquired did I have any others for sale. 'Why, hell yes,' I said, and hauled them out. He took five, including the one that was in the window—three big and two small—and wrote me out a check for four hundred dollars."

This windfall had a bad effect on Ellery. When he started his next painting, he found that he couldn't get anything to look right. Halfway through, he gave it up and started another. "I know now what was wrong," he says. "Instead of painting a picture for the fun of it, just something to show to Ma and the fellows on the dock, I was trying to paint a picture worth one hundred dollars." After a number of false starts, he lost his confidence. He wrapped his art gear in a blanket and stowed it in the *Eleanor*'s spare bunk and didn't paint any more for three years. In the summer of 1934, a Stonington captain bought a new dragger and asked Ellery to paint a picture of it. "What'll you give me?" Ellery asked. The captain offered a box of cigars. "Make it a quart of Scotch and throw in the cost of the canvas," Ellery told him, "and I'll see what I can do." The captain agreed. Ellery got out a stretched canvas and propped it against a lobster trap on the dock and sat on another trap and went to work. "I was real fumbly at first," he says, "but I soon got my nerve back. Everybody around the dock dropped what they were doing and came and stood in back of me and told me how to do it, but I finished it that afternoon and it turned out good. The dragger was fresh off the ways, hadn't even been shook down, but I put her out on the high seas, fighting a storm. That tickled the captain. When I got through, two other captains made arrangements with me to paint their boats."

Since then, Ellery has painted between fifty and sixty draggers, trawlers, mackerel seiners, and lobster boats, and his price has advanced from a quart of Scotch to thirty-five dollars if the client is a Stonington man or seventy-five if he is a stranger. "I'm proud of my painting," Ellery says. "On the other hand, I'm sorry I ever started it. It's hard to satisfy a fishing captain and it gets harder and harder. You not only have to paint his boat as accurate as a blueprint, you have to put it in a storm, a terrible storm. They all insist on that. Like a captain said the other day, 'It's a good painting, Ellery, only I wish you'd put in a bolt of lightning striking the mast.' Each wants a worse storm than the others. It's got so if I was to paint a boat that looked as if there was a remote possibility it might make port, the captain would take offense." Except for his own work, Ellery doesn't have much interest in painting. Once, when the *Eleanor* was laid up in Newport by engine trouble, he and Frank and Charlie spent an afternoon in Providence and visited the museum at the Rhode Island School of Design. They had on their fishing clothes and felt ill at ease and stayed only a few minutes. "We couldn't get out of there fast enough," Ellery says. He sometimes seems to feel that his success as a painter is a joke he has played on the world. "Nearly about every fishing captain from Point Jude to New London has one of my paintings hung up in his home," Ellery says, "and every now and then, when I'm driving past those homes at night, I can't help saying to myself, 'Good God A'mighty! What have I done?'" Other paintings by Ellery hang in net lofts, chandleries, dock offices, and dockside saloons in eastern Connecticut fishing ports. Most of these are of the *Eleanor*. Bindloss, the dock proprietor, owns six. There is a Thompson in Fulton Market. It is owned by Jim Coyne, general manager of John Feeney, Inc., the firm to which Ellery ships his fish, and it hangs in the Feeney stall in the old Fishmongers Association shed. Every summer, people from New York City, on vacation in and around Stonington, buy some of Ellery's work. They never fail to inform him that he is a primitive. This word used to anger him. He now understands its significance in relation to painting, but he pretends that he doesn't. Last summer, a woman from New York told him that she knew dozens of painters but he was the first primitive she'd ever met. "I'm not as primitive as I have been," Ellery said. "Nowheres near. Back before I got the rheumatism, I was without a doubt the most primitive man in eastern Connecticut."

. . .

The last few years, owing to the growth of his interest in oceanography, Ellery has been devoting less and
less time to painting. He says he first heard of
oceanography one Saturday afternoon in May, 1943.
He and several other dragger captains had called it a
week and were sitting in the sun on the stringpiece of
Bindloss's dock, sharing a bottle, when two strangers
walked up and introduced themselves: they were
Daniel Merriman, director of the Bingham Oceanographic Laboratory at Yale, and Herbert E. Warfel, a
research assistant. Mr. Merriman told the captains
that the staff of the laboratory was about to begin
work on a lengthy study of the fishes in the eastern
Connecticut and western Rhode Island grounds, and
he asked for their cooperation. He said that he and
Mr. Warfel would be in charge of the study and that
they wanted to drive over from New Haven once or
twice a month and go out to the grounds on
Stonington draggers and examine catches and make
oceanographic observations. When Ellery heard this,
he promptly left the group and went down the dock
and stayed in the cabin of the *Eleanor* until the
oceanographers had departed. Scientists of one sort
or another—aquatic biologists from the United
States Fish and Wildlife Service, ichthyologists from
New England universities, and, in recent years, drug-
company chemists assaying the vitamins in the liver

oil of various fishes—frequently visit the Stonington docks, and Ellery had formed a low opinion of them. On three occasions, just to be accommodating, he had taken scientists out to the Hell Hole. "They were all alike," he says. "The first hour, while we were making a drag, they got in the way. You couldn't turn around without stepping on Dr. Somebody-or-Other. The second hour, while we were sorting a haul, they sat on their tails and watched us sort and disputed among themselves concerning what was the right Latin name for this fish and that fish, and some-how—up to our knees in fish and wet to the skin—all that Latin had a tendency to get on our nerves. The third hour, they ate sandwiches. The fourth hour, they threw up."

The other captains were more sympathetic. That same month, Mr. Merriman and Mr. Warfel went out with Captain S. W. Stenhouse on the *Nathaniel B. Palmer* and with Captain W. H. McLaughlin on the *Marise.* During the first week of June, they went out with Captain Roscoe Bacchiocchi on the *Baby II.* Mr. Merriman noticed that these captains replied to a good many of the questions he and Mr. Warfel asked them by saying that they didn't know but that Captain Thompson, on the *Eleanor,* probably did. Captain Bacchiocchi, for example, when asked if hogchoker flounders ever entered Block Island Sound, said that he wouldn't know a hogchoker if he caught one but that he thought he remembered hearing Ellery Thompson say something or other about catching some. Twice, seeing the *Eleanor* tied up at Bindloss's dock, Mr. Merriman went aboard her looking for Captain Thompson, but each time a man down in the cabin, who he later found out was Captain Thompson himself, shouted up the companionway that Captain Thompson had just knocked off and gone to the movies. Finally, on a Sunday night late in June, Mr. Merriman telephoned Ellery at his home. Their conversation was an odd one, and Mr. Merriman can recollect it. He told Ellery that he was eager to make a trip to the grounds with him and started to tell why, but Ellery interrupted and asked, "What do you call yourself—Doctor or Mister?" Mr. Merriman said that he was a Ph.D. but much preferred to be called Mister. Ellery said he would have to think the matter over. Then, abruptly making up his mind, he said, "Oh, hell, be down at the dock tomorrow morning at half past five and we'll take you out and get it over with." Mr. Merriman tried to thank him, but Ellery interrupted again and said, "Don't thank me. Just keep out of the way. And when you see we've got our hands full pulling in a net and the dog-fish are swarming around and the gulls are screeching and the winch is backfiring and everything on deck is all balled up, don't you and the other professor pick that particular moment to butt in and ask questions.

And don't bring sandwiches. If there's anything I despise, it's sandwiches. While you're on my boat, I'll feed you."

Mr. Merriman, having known many fishing captains and having long since concluded that they are the most plainspoken of men, took Ellery's bluntness for granted. Mr. Merriman is a friendly, adaptable, serious young scientist who has put in about as much time in the field as in the laboratory. In 1930, deciding that fish interested him more than the liberal arts, he quit Harvard, where he was a junior, and spent two years knocking around fishing ports in the United States and England, going to banks in the Gulf of Maine in trawlers out of Groton and to banks in the North Sea in trawlers and herring drifters out of the English ports of Grimsby and Lowestoft. Then he returned to school—not to Harvard but to the College of Fisheries in the University of Washington, in Seattle. After getting a Master's degree at Washington for a study of the effects of temperature on the development of the eggs and larvae of the cutthroat trout, he went to Yale, in 1935, as a graduate student in zoology. In 1938, he became an instructor in biology. In 1942, when he was thirty-four, he was raised to assistant professor of biology, curator of oceanography in the Peabody Museum, and director of the Oceanographic Laboratory. A paper he did on the striped bass is the standard work on that fish. He is a Bostonian and a member of an old New England teaching family. His father, the late Professor Roger Bigelow Merriman, taught history at Harvard for forty-three years. Charles W. Eliot, the Harvard president, was an uncle.

Mr. Warfel is an Indianian of Pennsylvania Dutch descent. He has studied fish, sometimes as a teacher and sometimes as a state fish-and-game-department biologist, in Colorado, North Dakota, Oklahoma, Massachusetts, New Hampshire, and Connecticut. He believes that the proper study of fish embraces the cooking and eating of them. He originated a squid chowder. He and some of his colleagues occasionally stay late in the laboratory and make a quart of caviar, using eggs of the longhorn sculpin—the common hacklehead, a trash fish whose only value ordinarily is as bait for lobster traps.

Mr. Merriman and Mr. Warfel went out to the Hell Hole with Ellery on the last Monday in June, 1943. "Frank and I got down to the dock at five-thirty, as usual," Ellery says, "and the professors were already on the *Eleanor,* sitting on the hatch, making themselves at home, but Charlie hadn't showed up. The professors were sleepy-eyed and they hadn't bothered to shave and they had their old clothes on, and I mean old clothes. Frank and I went below to start the engine, and Frank said they were the most un-professor-looking two damned professors ever he saw. It was a hot, drizzly morning and Frank was cranky, and so was I. We got things started, but still no Charlie. Finally, the landlady of a rooming house up on Water Street that Charlie roomed with at that time's little boy came poking down the dock and said Charlie sent word he wasn't able to get out of bed, his left knee was hurting him so. Charlie's got something chronic the matter with his left knee, and he has to quit work every so often and doctor it. It's a peculiar affliction. It hardly ever troubles him until Saturday. Along about noon Saturday, he starts to limp around and look blue and complain his left knee is swoll up, and Saturday night he starts taking something to bring the swelling down. Sometimes it's Tuesday or Wednesday before the swelling goes down sufficient for him to do a day's work. He's tried all kinds of patent medicines and salves and liniments, but the only thing that seems to give him any real relief is rye whiskey. He takes it internally. I asked him one day, 'Charlie, for the love of God,' I said, 'why don't you try rubbing it on?,' but he said it seems to do more good if he takes it internally.

"I didn't much want to go out to the grounds without Charlie. We can work the *Eleanor* two-handed, but I don't like to; I'm one draggerman that aims to reach old age without wearing a truss. The professors spoke up and said they'd be glad to pitch in and help. I thought to myself, 'A lot of help you two'll be.' On the other hand, I wanted to keep my promise, so I told Frank to let's get going. I took her out past Watch Hill Light; then I gave Frank the wheel and I went below and got breakfast. I made some coffee and scrambled some eggs and I broiled four nice hen lobsters. As it happened, it was the first time the professors ever et lobsters for breakfast, but I didn't hear any complaints. We hit the Hell Hole and started to set the net and got in trouble right away. Frank shoved the bag of the net off the stern, the way he always does, but a wave caught it before it sank and gave it a throwing around, and that jerked the wings of the net sideways on the deck, and the bridle on one of the net doors got all snaked up. In other words, a damned mess. I was at the wheel and couldn't do anything about it. Frank ran back to try and fix it, but before he got there, Mr. Merriman leaped on the door and grabbed the bridle. I thought to myself, 'That's one young man that wasn't present when the brains was passed out,' and I yelled to him to stand back there. I fully expected to see him snatched into the middle of next week, but he seesawed the bridle back into working order as good as I could have done, or Frank, or any other dragger-man, and he leaped off the door a second or two before it went overboard like a shot out of a gun. I called him over to the wheel and I inquired where in hell did he learn how to handle an otter trawl. I asked him did they teach that up at Yale. And he said he'd worked in fishing boats to some extent when he was younger. So, naturally, when I heard that, I had some respect for him.

"When we brought the net in and emptied it on deck, the professors helped us sort. They squatted down and took right hold. There was all the difference in the world between them and the other scientists: They worked as hard as us, except for stopping now and then to jot down a note. And they didn't throw any Latin around. They used fishermen's fish names. They didn't call a squirrel hake a *Hippogloppus hoppogloppus;* they called it a snot head, the same as we do. We got the haul sorted and barreled, and then we went below for a mug-up, and they started in asking me questions such as did I ever come across any hogchokers, and when was the last bluefish run and how did it compare with the big bluefish runs in the old days, the bluefish gluts, and what species did I consider were being fished out, and other questions like that. They must've asked me fifty questions.

"We made two one-hour drags, and then a drizzly fog set in, so we proceeded back to the dock. We unloaded, and it was only noon, so I asked the professors why didn't they stay for lunch, I'd broil them a fluke. While we were eating, I told them it was my time to be district attorney, I'd like to ask *them* a question. I told them there was a matter that had bothered me since childhood days, that I had turned it over in my head a hundred times without coming to a sensible conclusion—namely, 'How do lobsters mate? How in the world do they manage it?' I asked did they know. Well, they knew. They had the scientific facts, and they got out their notepads and drew some diagrams to show the ABCs of the matter. Frank was up on deck, airing out a net, and I yelled to him to come below; I didn't want him to miss it. And that led to the mating habits of whales. And then I asked what was their private theories on the eelgrass mystery. That's a grass that used to grow on the bottom of bays all over the North Atlantic coast, thousands upon thousands of acres of it. It had long, narrow blades that looked eely. It was highly beneficial to fishermen, because scallops lived in it; it was shelter for the scallops. During 1931, it all disappeared. One week there'd be a thick stand of eelgrass in a bay; next week you couldn't find a living blade of it. Bay scallops practically disappeared, too. That's why they're so dear. The old retired fishermen sitting on the docks thought up all kinds of theories at the time, the way they do. One old man, an old Baptist, it was his idea that God was punishing the fishermen for their misspent lives. 'The eelgrass is only the beginning,' he used to say. 'The fish'll go next.' The professors had the facts. A fungus had got into the tissues of the grass—one of those buggers that can't be seen with the naked eye—and had multiplied to a God-awful extent. They made some sketches of it, how it looks under the microscope, and they explained how it rotted the grass. And then we got on the subject of the grounds in the Sargasso Sea, where the eels go to spawn, the American eels bedding down together in one ground and the European eels in another. And then we discussed the tides and the moon and the Gulf Stream and the Continental Shelf and the Continental Slope and the deeps. We talked and drank coffee all afternoon. I answered their questions and they answered mine. I gave them the practical dope and they gave me the scientific dope. It was quite a discussion and I really enjoyed it. When they were leaving, they asked could they go out again on the *Eleanor,* and I told them, 'Why, hell yes.' And they asked could they bring some of their apparatus aboard next trip, and I told them I didn't see any reason why not, they were entirely welcome to do so. I told them they could make the *Eleanor* their headquarters."

Ever since then, Mr. Merriman and Mr. Warfel have spent at least one day a month on the *Eleanor;* it has become their research vessel. Ellery has an old Yale pennant, a souvenir of a Yale-Harvard boat race at New London, that he flies when they are aboard. The oceanographers keep a number of reference books in the *Eleanor*'s pilothouse. In addition, one shelf of the canned-goods cupboard in the cabin is crammed with books, most of which are about fish. These belong to Ellery; he is building a scientific library of his own. He started it with *Fishes of the Gulf of Maine,* by Henry B. Bigelow and William W. Welsh, an old United States Bureau of Fisheries reference work that is a classic of American ichthyology. Mr. Merriman and Mr. Warfel found a copy for Ellery in a secondhand bookstore in Boston and gave it to him for Christmas in 1944. Ellery has great respect for it. He has read and reread it, he lends it to other captains, and he frequently quotes from it. Mr. Warfel believes that Ellery is no longer hostile to Latin and is quite sure that he has memorized the Latin fish names in Bigelow & Welsh. Ellery profanely denies this. He slips up every so often, however. Two sharks appear in multitudes in the Stonington grounds at certain seasons, the spiny dogfish *(Squalus acanthias)* and the smooth dogfish *(Mustelus canis).* Not long ago, in conversation with Mr. Warfel, Ellery mentioned a big shark that swam up while the net was coming out of the water and tore a hole in it trying to get at the fish inside, and Mr. Warfel asked, "What was it—a spiny dog or a smooth dog?" "It was an *acanthias,*" Ellery said.

Ellery and the oceanographers have become good friends. He calls them Dan and Herb. In between their trips to Stonington, he sends them logs, which are full of information about conditions on the grounds. He has collected many specimens for them. Whenever a Stonington draggerman notices a queer fish in a haul, such as one of the strays from tropical waters that work their way north in the Gulf Stream, he saves it and gives it to Ellery. Ellery writes the date and place of capture, and any other relevant facts the draggerman can supply, on a strip of rag paper, sticks this in the fish's mouth, and drops the fish in a five-gallon can of formaldehyde that the oceanographers keep in Bindloss's dock house for this purpose. The oceanographers have finished half a dozen monographs on phases of their study. In each of these, they acknowledged Ellery's assistance. For example, in a footnote in "The Spawning Habits, Eggs, and Larvae of the Sea Raven, *Hemitripterus americanus,* in Southern New England," they wrote, "The authors are greatly indebted to Captain Ellery Thompson of the vessel *Eleanor,* out of Stonington, Connecticut, whose cooperation has been invaluable in much of the work of this laboratory in recent years." Two of Ellery's paintings of the *Eleanor* have been acquired by the laboratory. Mr. Merriman and Mr. Warfel occasionally bring a colleague along on their trips to the grounds. Dr. Ernest Freeman Thompson, an international authority on the hermit crab, and Dr. Werner Bergmann, a chemistry professor who studies the taxonomy of marine invertebrates for fun, have made three trips each. Mr. Merriman's father once came down from Harvard and went out to the Mussel Bed with Ellery. All the way out, he stood by the wheel and told Ellery stories about Suleiman the Magnificent, of whom he had written a biography. Ellery liked him. When Professor Merriman died, in September of 1945, Ellery sent flowers. "He had a good head on him," Ellery says. After their monthly trip, Ellery always gives a supper for the oceanographers at his home in New London. At first, he just had cold cuts and beer, but his mother considered that inhospitable. Mrs. Thompson is a cook in the old American big-kitchen tradition, the kind of woman who will make a fruit or meringue pie that no pastry chef in New York City could equal and then apologize for it. She likes to cook and she likes to see people eat, and Ellery's suppers have developed into banquets. For a recent one, Mrs. Thompson stuffed a twenty-pound turkey with three dozen Robbins Island oysters and roasted it.

Mr. Merriman and Mr. Warfel drive over to Stonington in an old truck that the Oceanographic Laboratory shares with the geology department, and park it on Bindloss's dock. They bring two chests of apparatus—thermometers, silk plankton nets, Mason jars for small specimens, a measuring board, and a jug of formaldehyde. They set the chests up on the *Eleanor*'s aft hatch. During a drag, they bottle samples of sea water, surface and bottom; take the temperature of the air and of the water, surface and bottom; make weather notes; and collect samples of plankton, the microscopic floating plant and animal life that is the basic food of most fishes. When the net is brought aboard and emptied on deck, they examine a few members of each species of fish in the haul. Twenty-three species are encountered in numbers in the Stonington grounds. Commercially, they fall into three categories—regularly marketed, occasionally marketed, and trash. Eight species are regularly marketed—blackback flounders, yellowtail flounders, fluke flounders, witch flounders, cod, haddock, cunners, and porgies. Five species are occasionally marketed—windowpane flounders, whiting, Boston hake, squirrel hake, and ocean pout. Ten species are regarded as trash—Baptist flounders, longhorn sculpin, little skates, big skates, barn-door skates, goosefish, sea ravens, sea robins, spiny dogfish, and smooth dogfish. These are always sorted out and thrown back, a process that kills a large proportion of them. By accumulating data on the whole hauls of the *Eleanor* and of other draggers over a period of seven months, a project in which they were assisted by Ellery, Mr. Merriman and Mr. Warfel determined that approximately fifty-three per cent of the catch of the Stonington fleet is thrown back. They consider this an appalling waste. All these fish are edible, but

Americans are prejudiced against them, mainly because of their appearance; with the exception of the Baptist flounder, which has four lovely circle-within-a-circle designs on its top side, they are remarkably grotesque. In flavor and texture, most of them are as good as those that are regularly marketed, and one, the barn-door skate, when properly cooked, is superior. Skates are esteemed in England, and *raie au beurre noir* is one of the great fish dishes of France. Other New England fleets ship trash fish in small quantities to Fulton Market, where they are sold to two dissimilar groups: buyers for luxury hotels and restaurants, and proprietors of little one- and two-bin fish stores in Italian, Spanish, and Chinese neighborhoods.

A hodgepodge of invertebrates comes up in every dragger haul—lobsters, squid, blue crabs, rock crabs, hermit crabs, surf clams, blood clams, bay scallops, sea scallops, cockles, mussels, moon snails, pear conchs, sand dollars, starfish, serpent stars, sea anemones, sea squirts, sea mice, sea urchins, and sponges. Except for the lobsters and scallops, and sometimes the squid and blue crabs, these are also thrown back or swept through the scuppers—another example of blind American waste. The ripe raw roe of sea urchins is finer than most of the caviar that reaches us. Pear conchs, or conks, shipped as a sideline by oystermen and clammers, are used in a hot Italian dish called *scungili;* there are basement restaurants on Mulberry Street that specialize in it and are referred to as *scungili* places. *Scungili* is similar in taste and texture to mushrooms. Also, like mushrooms, it has a musky, wet-earth smell. People who go often to Italian restaurants have probably eaten pear conchs and moon snails without knowing it; both are widely used in a sauce for spaghetti and other *pasta* dishes. The Chinese in Chinatown use pear conchs in a number of dishes.

On every trip on the *Eleanor,* Mr. Merriman and Mr. Warfel pick out one haul, usually the second of the day, and buy all the fish in it, marketable and trash, paying whatever prices are current in Fulton Market. These fish, unsorted, are barreled and iced and set aside in the hold; there may be anywhere from two to six barrels. At the end of the trip, they are loaded on the truck and taken to the laboratory. Next day, Mr. Merriman and Mr. Warfel and their colleagues assemble around cutting tables in a room in the basement of the laboratory called the "crud room" and weigh and measure and decipher the sex of every fish. Samples of each species are then put in cold storage and taken out one by one and dissected and examined in regard to age, stage of sexual maturity, stomach contents, and parasites—a job that takes several days. This laboratory data and the data collected on the grounds, when put together, like the parts of a puzzle, yield information about spawning and feeding habits, rates of growth, ages, natural and fishing mortalities, fish diseases, competition among fishes for food, and relationships between individuals and between species. An analysis of the causes of fluctuations in abundance in southern New England fishing grounds will be made on the basis of this information. That is the main purpose of the study. The oceanographers hope that they will eventually be able to estimate the tonnage of each species that draggermen can take in a season without dangerously depleting the stock.

Fishermen and fishmongers along the southern New England coast have given obscene names to a number of fishes. Some of these names are so imaginative, scornful, and apt that they are startling. Mr. Merriman and Mr. Warfel collect them. They also collect Block Island Stories, or Block Islands. Block Island is nine miles out in the Atlantic, off Rhode Island, to which it belongs; it is small and shaped like an oyster shell and almost treeless. The tides around it are treacherous, and hundreds of ships have been wrecked on its reefs and sand bars. The islanders are cold to strangers and are hostile to fishermen from the mainland who drag in the grounds surrounding it, such as the Hell Hole and the Mussel Bed. In retaliation, the mainlanders for generations have made up stories about them, accusing them of stinginess and of depending upon wrecks for a living.

One midwinter afternoon, the *Eleanor,* with the oceanographers aboard, skirted Cow Cove, on the northern tip of Block Island, while returning from a trip to the Mussel Bed. It was a sunny, still afternoon, and the air was so clear that the lighthouse on Montauk Point, twenty miles to the southwest, was visible. Frank was at the wheel. Ellery and Mr. Merriman and Mr. Warfel were sitting on the aft hatch, eating boiled lobsters. Charlie was lying on his back in the life dory, staring at a photograph in a magazine called *Sunshine and Health,* which is the official organ of the American Sunbathing Association, a nudist group. Next to *Popular Mechanics,* it is his favorite magazine. Ellery suddenly snapped his fingers. "I was about to forget," he said. "I heard a Block Island the other day. Johnny Bindloss told it. Johnny had it years ago from his grandfather, old man William Park Bindloss. He was a stonemason who specialized in lighthouses. He built South East Light on Block Island, and he lived over there a year or two and got acquainted. In those days, according to the general talk, the islanders got the better part of their bread and butter salvaging off wrecks. There'd be wrecks on the reefs all during the winter, coasting vessels mostly, and the stuff in them would wash up on the beach. The islanders would stand on the beach

all day and all night, hooking for the stuff with poles
that had bent nails on the ends of them. They were
called wreck hooks. Everybody would line up down
there and hook—little children, great-grandmoth-
ers, *every*body that could walk. The competition got
so thick that they all agreed on a standard-length
hook. Everybody had to use the same length. Around
that time, a preacher from the mainland came over
and settled on the island to preach the word of God
and make a living for himself. The islanders listened
to him, but they didn't offer to pay him anything.
Along about February, he got real lean and raggedy.
He was nothing but skin and bones. The islanders
didn't want him to starve to death over there. For
one thing, they'd have to bury him. So they held a
meeting and argued the matter back and forth. One
man made a motion they should take up a collection
for the preacher, but this man had a reputation for
being simple and his motion was so idiotic they didn't
even discuss it. Some wanted each family to give the
preacher a peck of potatoes or a turnip or two, and
some were for giving him a fish whenever there was
a good big catch, a glut. They couldn't agree. They
argued until late that night. Finally, they decided
they'd let him have a wreck hook an inch and a half
longer than all the rest. If he couldn't make a living
with that, he could go ahead and starve to death."

"Take the wheel a few minutes, Ellery, if you don't mind," said Frank, "and I'll tell a Block Island."

Ellery got up and relieved Frank, who came over and sat on the hatch.

"There was a fisherman from Stonington named Tucker Seabury who used to go over to Block Island and fish for cod a month or two every fall," Frank said. "Did it for years and years. Tuck was an old bachelor, and sort of odd himself. He got to know the Block Islanders, and they got to know him. In fact, he and the Block Islanders gradually got to be quite friendly. Tuck was what you call an old hand-liner. He'd go out in a dory and kneel over the side and fish for cod with hand lines. They don't fish much that way any more. He mostly fished on the Ledge. That's a hidden reef that juts out from the island a considerable distance. There's a buoy anchored off the end of it. Tuck was out there on the reef one afternoon in his dory, the way he used to tell it, and the cod were running and he was busy as Billy be damned and after a while he happened to look up and he saw a schooner heading for the reef, a big coasting schooner. It was coming in between the buoy and the island, taking a shortcut. It was an insane sight. Tuck stood up in his dory and waved both arms and screamed. 'Reef!' he screamed. 'Reef! Reef! Reef! Good God A'mighty, you're heading for a reef!' The schooner turned aside and shot out past the buoy, just in time. A few yards more and there'd've been an awful, awful wreck. Tuck glanced toward the landing on the island and there was a crowd of Block Islanders standing there, men and women, watching. Tuck was quite pleased with himself. He figured the Block Islanders would praise him for the good deed he had done. On toward sundown, he rowed in. The crowd of Block Islanders was still on the landing, standing around. Tuck nodded and spoke, the same as he always did, but the Block Islanders didn't speak. They just stood and looked at him. There was an old man among them who had always been Tuck's best friend on the island. Finally, this old man gave Tuck a cold look and said, 'Why don't you mind your own business?' "

Charlie laid aside his *Sunshine and Health* and sat up in the life dory. "That must've been around the time old Christine was ruling the south end of the island," Charlie said. "Old Chrissy was an old rascal of a woman that was the head of a gang of wreckers. They lured ships in with false lights, and they killed the sailors and passengers, so there wouldn't be any tales told. Old Chrissy always took charge of the killing. She had a big club and she'd hist her skirt and wade out in the surf and clout the people on the head as they swam in or floated in. She called a wreck a wrack, the way the Block Islanders do. That's the way she pronounced it. One night, she and her gang lured a ship up on the reef, and the sailors were floating in, and old Chrissy was out there clouting them on their heads. One poor fellow floated up, and it was one of old Chrissy's sons, who'd left the island and gone to the mainland to be a sailor. He looked up at old Chrissy and said, 'Hello, Ma.' Old Chrissy didn't hesitate a moment. She lifted up her club and clouted him on the head. 'A son's a son,' she said, 'but a wrack's a wrack.' "

(1947)

The Rivermen

I often feel drawn to the Hudson River, and I have spent a lot of time through the years poking around the part of it that flows past the city. I never get tired of looking at it; it hypnotizes me. I like to look at it in midsummer, when it is warm and dirty and drowsy, and I like to look at it in January, when it is carrying ice. I like to look at it when it is stirred up, when a northeast wind is blowing and a strong tide is running—a new-moon tide or a full-moon tide—and I like to look at it when it is slack. It is exciting to me on weekdays, when it is crowded with ocean craft, harbor craft, and river craft, but it is the river itself that draws me, and not the shipping, and I guess I like it best on Sundays, when there are lulls that sometimes last as long as half an hour, during which, all the way from the Battery to the George Washing- ton Bridge, nothing moves upon it, not even a ferry, not even a tug, and it becomes as hushed and dark and secret and remote and unreal as a river in a dream. Once, in the course of such a lull, on a Sunday morning in April, 1950, I saw a sea sturgeon rise out of the water. I was on the New Jersey side of the river that morning, sitting in the sun on an Erie Railroad coal dock. I knew that every spring a few sturgeon still come in from the sea and go up the river to spawn, as hundreds of thousands of them once did, and I had heard tugboatmen talk about them, but this was the first one I had ever seen. It was six or seven feet long, a big, full-grown sturgeon. It rose twice, and cleared the water both times, and I plainly saw its bristly snout and its shiny little eyes and its white belly and its glistening, greenish-yellow, bony-plated, crocodilian back and sides, and it was a spooky sight.

I prefer to look at the river from the New Jersey side; it is hard to get close to it on the New York side, because of the wall of pier sheds. The best points of vantage are in the riverfront railroad yards in Jersey City, Hoboken, and Weehawken. I used to disregard the "DANGER" and "RAILROAD PROPERTY" and "NO TRESPASSING" signs and walk into these yards and wander around at will. I would go out to the end of one of the railroad piers and sit on the stringpiece and stare at the river for hours, and nobody ever bothered me. In recent years, however, the railroad police and pier watchmen have become more and more inquisitive. Judging from the questions they ask, they suspect every stranger hanging around the river of spying for Russia. They make me uneasy. Several years ago, I began going farther up the river, up to Edgewater, New Jersey, and I am glad I did, for I found a new world up there, a world I never knew existed, the world of the rivermen.

Edgewater is across the river from the upper West Side of Manhattan; it starts opposite Ninety-fourth Street and ends opposite 164th Street. It is an unusually narrow town. It occupies a strip of stony land between the river and the Palisades, and it is three and a half miles long and less than half a mile wide at its widest part. The Palisades tower over it, and overshadow it. One street, River Road, runs the entire length of it, keeping close to the river, and is the main street. The crosstown streets climb steeply from the bank of the river to the base of the Palisades, and are quite short. Most of them are only two blocks long, and most of them are not called streets but avenues or terraces or places or lanes. From these streets, there is a panoramic view of the river and the Manhattan skyline. It is a changeable view, and it is often spectacular. Every now and then—at daybreak, at sunset, during storms, on starry summer nights, on hazy Indian-summer afternoons,

on blue, clear-cut, stereoscopic winter afternoons—
it is astonishing.

The upper part of Edgewater is largely residential. This is the oldest part of town, and the narrow-
est, but it still isn't entirely built up. There are several
stretches of trees and underbrush, and several bushy
ravines running down to the river, and a number of
vacant lots. The lots are grown up in weeds and
vines, and some of them are divided by remnants of
stone walls that once divided fields or pastures. The
streets are lined with old trees, mostly sweet gums
and sycamores and tulip trees. There are some
wooden tenements and some small apartment houses
and some big old blighted mansions that have been
split up into apartments, but one-family houses pre-
dominate. The majority are two-story houses, many
of them set back in good-sized yards. Families try to
outdo each other in landscaping and ornamenting
their yards, and bring home all sorts of odds and ends
for the purpose; in yard after yard conventional garden ornaments such as sundials and birdbaths and
wagon wheels painted white stand side by side with
objects picked up around the riverfront or rescued
during the demolition of old buildings. The metal
deckhouse of an old Socony tanker barge is in the
front yard of one house on River Road; it is now a
garden shed. In the same yard are a pair of mooring

bitts, a cracked stone eagle that must have once been on the façade of a public building or a bank, and five of those cast-iron stars that are set in the walls of old buildings to cap the ends of strengthening rods. In the center of a flower bed in one yard is a coalhole cover and in the center of a flower bed in an adjoining yard is a manhole cover. In other yards are old anchors and worm wheels and buoys and bollards and propellers. Edgewater used to be linked to Manhattan by a ferry, the Edgewater–125th Street ferry. Most of the captains, wheelsmen, and deckhands on the ferryboats were Edgewater men, and had been for generations, and the ferry was the pride of the town. It stopped running in 1950; it was ruined by the George Washington Bridge and the Lincoln Tunnel. There are relics of it in a dozen yards. In former Mayor Henry Wissel's yard, on Hilliard Avenue, there is a chain post that came off the vehicle gangway of the ferryboat *Shadyside,* and the *Shadyside*'s fog bell hangs beside his door. In former Fire Chief George Lasher's yard, on Undercliff Avenue, there is a hookup wheel that came off the landing stage of the old ferryhouse. It resembles a ship's wheel. Chief Lasher has painted it white, and has trained a climbing rose on it.

In the middle of Edgewater, around and about River Road and the foot of Dempsey Avenue, where the ferryhouse used to stand, there is a small business district. In addition, a few stores and a few neighborhood saloons of the type known in New Jersey as taverns are scattered along River Road in the upper and lower parts of town.

The lower part of Edgewater is called Shadyside; the ferryboat was named for it. It is a mixed residential and factory district. The majority of the factories are down close to the river, in a network of railroad sidings, and piers jut out from them. Among them are an Aluminum Company of America factory, a coffee-roasting plant, a factory that makes roofing materials, a factory that makes sulphuric acid, and a factory that makes a shortening named Spry. On the roof of the Spry factory is an enormous electric sign; the sign looms over the river, and on rainy, foggy nights its pulsating, endlessly repeated message, "SPRY FOR BAKING," "SPRY FOR BAKING," "SPRY FOR BAKING," seems to be a cryptic warning of some kind that New Jersey is desperately trying to get across to New York.

There are six or seven large factories in Shadyside and six or seven small ones. The Aluminum Company factory is by far the largest, and there is something odd about it. It is made up of a group of connecting buildings arranged in a U, with the prongs of the U pointed toward the river, and inside the U, covering a couple of acres, is an old cemetery. This is the Edgewater Cemetery. Most of the old families in

Edgewater have plots in it, and some still have room in their plots and continue to bury there. The land on which Edgewater is situated and the land for some distance along the river above and below it was settled in the seventeenth century by Dutch and Huguenot farmers. Their names are on the older gravestones in the cemetery—Bourdettes and Vreelands and Bogerts and Van Zandts and Wandells and Dyckmans and Westervelts and Demarests. According to tradition, the Bourdette family came in the sixteen-thirties—1638 is the date that is usually specified—and was the first one there; the name is now spelled Burdette or Burdett. Some of the families came over from Manhattan and some from down around Hoboken. They grew grain on the slopes, and planted orchards in the shelter of the Palisades. In the spring, during the shad and sturgeon runs, they fished, and took a large part of their catch to the city. The section was hard to get to, except by water, and it was rural and secluded for a long time. In the early eighteen-hundreds, some bluestone quarries were opened, and new people, most of whom were English, began to come in and settle down and intermarry with the old farming and fishing families. They were followed by Germans, and then by Irish straight from Ireland. Building stones and paving blocks and curbing for New York City were cut in the quarries and carried to the city on barges—paving blocks from Edgewater are still in place, under layers of asphalt, on many downtown streets. Some of the new people worked in the quarries, some worked on the barges, some opened blacksmith shops and made and repaired gear for the quarries and the barges, some opened boatyards, and some opened stores. The names of dozens of families who were connected with these enterprises in one way or another are on gravestones in the newer part of the cemetery; Allison, Annett, Carlock, Cox, Egg, Forsyth, Gaul, Goetchius, Hawes, Hewitt, Jenkins, Stevens, Truax, and Winterburn are a few. Some of these families died out, some moved away, and some are still flourishing. The enterprises themselves disappeared during the first two decades of this century; they were succeeded by the Shadyside factories.

The land surrounding the Edgewater Cemetery was once part of a farm owned by the Vreeland family, and the Aluminum Company bought this land from descendants of a Winterburn who married a Vreeland. As a condition of the sale, the company had to agree to provide perpetual access to the cemetery. To reach it, funerals go through the truck gate of the factory and across a freight yard and up a cement ramp. It is a lush old cemetery, and peaceful, even though the throb of machinery can be felt in every corner of it. A part-time caretaker does a good deal of gardening in it, and he likes bright colors. For borders, he uses the same gay plants that are used in flower beds at race tracks and seaside hotels—cannas, blue hydrangeas, scarlet sage, and cockscomb. Old men and old women come in the spring, with hoes and rakes, and clean off their family plots and plant old-fashioned flowers on them. Hollyhocks are widespread. Asparagus has been planted here and there, for its feathery ferny sprays. One woman plants sunflowers. Coarse, knotty, densely tangled rosebushes grow on several plots, hiding graves and gravestones. The roses that they produce are small and fragile and extraordinarily fragrant, and have waxy red hips almost as big as crab apples. Once, walking through the cemetery, I stopped and talked with an old woman who was down on her knees in her family plot, setting out some bulbs at the foot of a grave, and she remarked on the age of the rosebushes. "I believe some of the ones in here now were in here when I was a young woman, and I am past eighty," she said. "My mother—this is her grave—used to say there were rosebushes just like these all over this section when she was a girl. Along the riverbank, beside the roads, in people's yards, on fences, in waste places. And she said her mother—that's her grave over there—told her she had heard from *her* mother that all of them were descended from one bush that some poor uprooted woman who came to this country back in the Dutch times potted up and brought along with her. There used to be a great many more in the cemetery than there are now—they overran everything—and every time my mother visited the cemetery she would stand and look at them and kind of laugh. She thought they were a nuisance. All the same, for some reason of her own, she admired them, and enjoyed looking at them. 'I know why they do so well in here,' she'd say. 'They've got good strong roots that go right down into the graves.'"

The water beside several of the factory piers in Shadyside has been deepened by dredging to depths ranging between twenty and thirty feet. Everywhere else along Edgewater the inshore water is shallow. Off the upper part of town are expanses of shoals that are called the Edgewater Flats. They are mucky, miry, silty, and oily. Stretches of them are exposed at low tide, or have only a foot or two of water over them. In some places, they go out two hundred yards before they reach a depth of six feet. For generations, the Edgewater Flats have been a dumping ground for wrecks. Out in them, lying every which way, as if strewn about long ago by a storm, are the ruins of scores of river vessels. Some of these vessels were replaced by newer vessels and laid up in the flats against a time that they might possibly be used again, and that time never came. Some got out of commission and weren't worth repairing, and were towed into the flats and stripped of their metal and abandoned. Some had leaks, some had fires, and some had collisions. At least once a day, usually when the tide is at or around dead ebb, flocks of harbor gulls suddenly appear and light on the wrecks and scavenge the refuse that has collected on them during the rise and fall of the tide, and for a little while they crawl with gulls, they become white and ghostly with gulls, and then the gulls leave as suddenly as they came. The hulks of three ferryboats are out in the flats—the *Shadyside,* the *George Washington,* and the old *Fort Lee.* Nothing is left of the *Shadyside* but a few of her ribs and part of her keel. There are old tugboats out there, and old dump scows, and old derrick lighters, and old car floats. There are sand-and-gravel barges, and brick barges, and stone barges, and coal barges, and slaughterhouse barges. There are five ice barges out there, the last of a fleet that used to bring natural ice down to New York City from the old icehouse section along the west shore of the river, between Saugerties and Coxsackie. They have been in the flats since 1910, they are waterlogged, and they sit like hippopotamuses in the silt.

Close to shore are some barges that are still being used. They are drawn up in a straggly row, facing the shore, and narrow, zigzaggy footwalks built on piles made of drift lumber go out to them. These are second-hand railroad barges. They were once owned by the Pennsylvania, the Erie, the New York Central, the Jersey Central, and other railroads that operate barge fleets in the harbor. Their bottoms are sound and their roofs are tight, but they got too old to be jerked this way and that by tugs in a hurry and bumped about and banged into (most of them are over forty years old, and several are over sixty), so they were discarded and sold. Some are owned by shadfishermen, who move them up or down the river at the start of the shad season and tie them up along the bank, each fisherman placing his barge as close as possible to his row of nets. The fishermen eat and sleep aboard them and use them as bases while the shad are running, and then return them to the flats and keep them there the rest of the year and store their equipment in them. Others are owned by boat clubs. There are seven boat clubs on the Edgewater riverfront, and four are quartered in secondhand railroad barges. One club, the Undercliff Motor Boat Club, owns two, but uses both for the winter storage of its boats, and has its quarters in an old queen of an oyster barge named the *G. M. Still.* The wholesale oyster companies in New York City used to carry on their businesses in specially built barges that were docked the year round at piers on the East River, just north of Fulton Fish Market. These barges had two or three decks, and could hold huge stocks of oysters. They were top-heavy but beautifully made.

Some had balconies with banisters shaped like ten-pins on their upper decks, and the offices in several had mahogany paneling; the reputation of an oyster company partly depended on the splendor of its barge. There were over a dozen oyster barges on the East River at one time, and all were painted a variety of colors and all had ostentatious black-and-gold nameboards across their fronts and all flew swallow-tail pennants; people visited the waterfront just to see them. The *G. M. Still* was the last to go. It was owned by George M. Still, Inc., the planters of Diamond Point oysters, and its final East River location was at a pier at the foot of Pike Street, under the Manhattan Bridge; it was there for a generation. In 1949, the city took over this pier, and the Still company was unable to find another, so it moved ashore, and sold the barge to a dealer in old boats, who sold it to the boat club. The *G. M. Still* is almost eighty years old—it was built in 1880—and the recent years have been hard on it. Even so, not all the teardrops, icicles, scallops, and other scroll-saw curlicues that once ornamented it have disappeared, and its last coat of paint under the Still ownership—black, yellow, white, orange, and green—has not entirely faded, and the balcony on the bow end of its upper deck looks as regal as ever.

Although Edgewater is only a short ride by sub-way and bus from the heart of New York City, it has some of the characteristics of an isolated and ingrown old town in New England or the South. The population is approximately four thousand, and a large proportion of the people are natives and know each other, at least to speak to. A surprising number of them are related, some so distantly that they aren't at all sure just how. The elderly people take a deep interest in local history, a good deal of which has been handed down from generation to generation by word of mouth, and nearly all of them who are natives consider themselves authorities on the subject. When these elderly people were young, quite a few men and women bearing the names of the original Dutch and Huguenot families were still living in old family mansions along River Road—one old man or one old woman living alone, as often as not, or, in some cases, two old bachelor brothers or two old spinster sisters living together, or an old woman living with a bachelor son or a spinster daughter—and they remember them. They know in a general way how the present-day old families are interrelated, and how several of these families are related to the original families. They can fish around in their memories and bring up vital statistics and stray facts and rumors and old jokes and sayings concerning a multitude of people who have been dead and gone for a generation, and can point out where buildings stood that have been torn down for fifty years. Sometimes, in the manner of old people in old towns, unable to tell only a little when they know so much, they respond to a simple question with a labyrinthine answer. One day, shortly after I began going up to Edgewater, I became acquainted with an elderly native named Henry R. Gaul, and went for a walk with him. Mr. Gaul is a retired oil-company executive. For many years, the Valvoline Oil Company operated a refinery on the riverbank in Shadyside, and Mr. Gaul was chief clerk there. He is secretary of the Undercliff Motor Boat Club and, to have something to do, he looks after the club's winter-storage barges and its headquarters barge, the old *G. M. Still.* His friends call him Henny. Walking on River Road, Mr. Gaul and I came to an automobile that had broken down. It was alongside the curb, and two men in greasy overalls were working on it. One had the hood up, and was bent over the engine. The other was underneath the automobile, flat on his back. As we were passing by, the man underneath thrust his head out, to say something to the man working on the engine. As he did so, he caught sight of Mr. Gaul. "Hello, Henny," he said.

Mr. Gaul was startled. He paused and turned and peered down at the man's face, and then said, "Oh, hello, Bill." "That was Bill Ingold," he said as we resumed our walk. "He runs the Edgewater Garage."

I was curious about the name; Mr. Gaul had

referred to several names as old Edgewater names, and I asked him if Ingold was another one of them.

"Ingold?" he said. "Well, I should hope to think it is. It isn't one of the old Dutch names, but it's old enough, and Bill's got some of the old Dutch blood in him anyhow, through his mother's people. Knickerbocker Dutch. Not that he'd ever mention it. That's the way it is in Edgewater. There's a number of people over here who have old, old families back behind them—much older, I dare say, than the families back behind a high percentage of the people in the *Social Register* in New York—but you'd never find it out from them. Bill's mother was a Bishop, and *her* mother was a Carlock. The old Dutch blood came down to him through the Carlocks. The Carlocks were big people over here once, but they had a preponderance of daughters and the name died out. They owned land, and one branch of them ran a boatyard. The boatyard was torn down years and years ago, but I can tell you where it stood. Did you ever notice an ancient old clapboard building on the upper part of River Road with a saloon in it named Sulyma's Bar & Grill? Well, in the old days that building was a hotel named the Buena Vista Hotel, only we called it Walsch's, after the family that ran it. And just before you got to Walsch's, on the right, in between River Road and the river, was Carlock's Boatyard.

Bill Ingold's father was also named Bill—William, that is, William F. He was in the Edgewater Fire Department. In fact, he was Fire Chief. He was a highly respected man, and I'll tell you a little story to illustrate that. There used to be an old gentleman in Edgewater named Frederick W. Winterburn. Mr. Winterburn was rich. He had inherited money, and he had married money, and he had made money. His wife was a Vreeland, and she was related to the Dyckmans *and* the Westervelts. Among other things, he owned practically the whole of Shadyside, and he lived down there. He lived in a big house overlooking the river, and he had a rose garden in front and an orchard in back. On warm summer nights, walking along River Road, you could smell the roses in his garden. And you could smell the peaches in his orchard, all soft and ripe and still warm from the sun and a little breeze blowing across them. And you could smell the grapes hanging on a fence between the garden and the orchard. They were fox grapes, and they had a musky smell. I'd give anything to smell those grapes again. The garden had marble statues in it. Statues of women. Naked woman. Naked marble women. Goddesses, I guess you'd call them. In the moonlight, they looked real. It's all gone now, and there's a factory there. One piece of Mr. Winterburn's property surrounded the Edgewater Cemetery. His parents were buried in this cemetery, and his wife's people all the way back to the seventeenth century were buried in there, and he knew he was going to be buried in there, and he took a personal interest in it. In 1909 or 1910 or thereabouts—it might've been a few years earlier or a few years later—Mr. Winterburn was beginning to have a feeling that time was running out on him, he wouldn't be here much longer, although to tell you the truth he lived quite a few years more, and one day he asked five men to come to his house. All of them were from old Edgewater families and had people buried in the cemetery, and one of them was Bill Ingold's father, Fire Chief Ingold. 'Sit down, boys,' Mr. Winterburn said, 'I want to talk to you. Boys,' he said, 'my family owns much more space in the cemetery than it'll ever need or make use of, and I'm going to set aside a section of it for a poor plot. Any bona fide resident of Edgewater who dies a pauper can be buried in this plot, free of charge. And suicides that are turned away by other cemeteries can be buried in there, provided they're residents. And nonresidents that drown in the river and wash up on the Edgewater riverfront and don't have any identification on them, the way it sometimes happens, it doesn't make any difference if it looks accidental or looks as if they threw themselves in, they can be buried in there. Furthermore, I'm going to set up a trust fund, and I'm going to fix it so the principal can't ever be touched, whereas the interest can be used in perpetuity to keep up the cemetery. And I want you boys to form a cemetery association and elect a president and a secretary and a treasurer, and the duties of these officers shall be to keep an eye on the cemetery and visit it every now and then and make a tour of inspection through it and hire a caretaker and see that he keeps the weeds cut and the leaves raked and whenever the occasion arises rule on who can be buried in the poor plot and who can't be.' So they put it to a vote, and Fire Chief Ingold was elected president without any discussion whatsoever. It was taken for granted. That's how respected he was. And after he died, Bill was elected president, and he's held the office ever since. Did I mention Bill's mother was a Bishop? Well, she was. The Bishops were . . ."

Some of the people in Edgewater commute to jobs in New York City, and some work in the river towns south of Edgewater, which are, in order, going south, North Bergen, Guttenberg, West New York, Weehawken, Hoboken, and Jersey City, but the majority work in the factories in Shadyside. A score or so of men are spoken of around town as rivermen. This word has a special shade of meaning in Edgewater: a riverman not only works on the river or kills a lot of time on it or near it, he is also emotionally attached to it—he can't stay away from it.

Charles Allison is an example. Mr. Allison lives in Edgewater and works in North Bergen. He is a partner in the Baldwin & Allison Dry Dock Co., a firm that operates a drydock and calks and repairs barges and drives piles and builds docks and does marine surveying and supplies pumps for salvage work, but that is only one of the reasons he is looked upon as a riverman. The main reason is that the river has a hold on him. Most days he is on or around it from early in the morning until sunset. Nevertheless, he often goes down to it at night and walks beside it. Even on Sundays and holidays, he often goes down to it. The offices of the drydock company are in a superstructure built on the deck of an old railroad barge that is permanently docked at a pier in North Bergen, and Mr. Allison has had big wide windows put in three of the walls of his private office, so that he can sit at his desk and see up, down, and across the river. Every spring, he takes a leave of absence from the drydock, and spends from six weeks to two months living aboard a shad barge on the river and fishing two rows of shad nets with a crew of hired fishermen.

Some men work full time on the river—on ferries, tugs, or barges—and are not considered rivermen; they are simply men who work on the river. Other men work only a part of the year on the river and make only a part of their living there but are considered rivermen. Mr. Ingold, the garage proprietor, is one of these. His garage is on River Road, facing the river. It is a typical small, drafty, one-story garage, except that hanging on its walls, in among the fan belts and the brake linings and the dented chromium hubcaps and the calendars with naked girls on them, are anchors and oars and hanks of netting and dozens of rusty old eelpots. Also, standing in a shallow box of sand in the middle of the floor is a stove of a kind that would be recognizable only to people who are familiar with harbor shipping; it is shaped like an oil drum and burns coke and is a kind that is used in barges and lighters to keep perishable freight from freezing. Mr. Ingold took it out of an old Erie Railroad fruit-and-vegetable barge. In the winter, a group of elderly Edgewater men, most of whom are retired, sit around it and gossip and argue; in the summer, they move their chairs up front to the door, where they can look out on the river and the Manhattan skyline. Mr. Ingold owns two shad barges and several shad boats, and keeps them at a landing a short walk up the river from the garage. Off and on during the winter, he and another riverman, Eustus R. Smith, stretch shad nets across the floor of the garage and put them in shape. They rig new nets, and mend and splice old ones. They are helped occasionally by Mr. Ingold's son, Willy, and by Mr. Smith's son, Charlie. In the spring, Mr. Ingold leaves the garage in the hands of two mechanics, and he and his son and Mr.

Smith and his son go out on the river and become shadfishermen for a couple of months. In the late fall and early winter, when the eels in the river are at their best and bring the highest prices, Mr. Ingold and Willy set eelpots. They set sixty, and their favorite grounds are up around Spuyten Duyvil, where the Harlem River runs into the Hudson. Some nights during the eel season, after knocking off work in the garage, Mr. Ingold gets in an outboard and goes up to Spuyten Duyvil and attends to the pots, drawing them up hand over hand from the bottom and taking out the trapped eels and putting in fresh bait, and some nights Willy goes up. On dark nights, they wear miner's caps that have head lamps on them. Mr. Ingold has been dividing his time between the garage and the river for thirty-five years. Invariably, at the end of the shad season he is so tired he has to hole up in bed for a few days, and he always resolves to stay put in the garage from then on—no man can serve two masters—but when the eel season comes around he always finds himself back on the river again.

The riverman I know best is an old-timer named Harry Lyons. Harry is seventy-four, and has been around the river all his life. He lives with his wife, Mrs. Juel Lyons, in a two-story frame-and-fieldstone house backed up against the base of the Palisades, on Undercliff Avenue, in the upper part of Edgewater.

He owns a shad barge and an assortment of boats, and keeps them anchored just off the riverbank, a few minutes' walk from his house. Harry is five feet six, and weighs a hundred and fifty. He is one of those short, hearty, robust men who hold themselves erect and swagger a little and are more imposing than many taller, larger men. He has an old-Roman face. It is strong-jawed and prominent-nosed and bushy-eyebrowed and friendly and reasonable and sagacious and elusively piratical. Ordinarily, down on the riverfront, he looks like a beachcomber: he wears old pants and a windbreaker and old shoes with slashes cut in them, and he goes bareheaded and his hair sticks straight up. One day, however, by chance, I ran into him on a River Road bus, and he was on his way to a funeral down in Weehawken, and he was wearing his Sunday clothes and his hair was brushed and his face was solemn, and I was surprised at how distinguished he looked; he looked worldly and cultivated and illustrious.

Harry spends a large part of his time wandering up and down the riverfront looking at the river, or sitting on his barge looking at the river, but he isn't lazy. He believes in first things first; if there is anything at home or on the barge that should be attended to, he goes ahead and attends to it, and then sits down. He is handy with tools, and has a variety of skills. He is a good fisherman, a good netmaker, a fairly good carpenter, a fairly good all-round mechanic, and an excellent fish cook. He is especially good at cooking shad, and is one of the few men left who know how to run an old-fashioned Hudson River shad bake. Shad bakes are gluttonous springtime blowouts that are held in the middle or latter part of the shad season, generally under the trees on the riverbank, near a shad barge. They are given by lodges and labor unions, and by business, social, political, and religious organizations, and by individuals. Former Mayor Wissel—he was Mayor of Edgewater for thirty years—used to give one every year for the public officials in Edgewater and nearby towns.

When Harry is engaged to run a bake, he selects a sufficient number of roe shad from his own nets and dresses them himself and takes the roes out of them. He has a shad boner come up from Fulton Fish Market and bone them. Then, using zinc roofing nails, he nails them spread-eagle fashion to white-oak planks, one fish to a plank; the planks are two feet long, a foot and a half wide, and an inch thick, and have adjustable props fixed to their sides so that it is possible to stand them upright or tilt them backward. He nails two or three strips of bacon across each fish. When it is time to cook the fish—they aren't baked, they are broiled—he props the planks up, fish-side foremost, in a ring around a bed of charcoal that has been burning on the ground for hours and is red-hot and radiant. He places the planks only six inches or so from the coals, but he gradually moves them farther back, so that the fish will broil slowly and pick up the flavors of the bacon and the oak; they broil for almost an hour. Every so often, he takes a turn around the ring and thoroughly mops each fish with a cotton mop, which he keeps dipping into a pot of melted butter. While Harry looks after the shad, Mrs. Lyons looks after the roes, cooking them in butter in huge frying pans. Pickled beets and new potatoes boiled in their skins are usually served with the shad and the roe. Paper plates are used. The people eat on tables made of boards laid across saw-horses, and are encouraged to have several helpings. Cooked shad-bake style by an expert, shad is crusty on the outside and tender and rich and juicy on the inside (but not too rich, since a good deal of the oil has been broiled out of it), and fully justifies its scientific name, *Alosa sapidissima,* the *"Alosa"* of which means "shad" and the *"sapidissima"* of which means "good to eat to a superlative degree." Shad bakes require a lot of work, and most of them are small affairs. Some years, the New Jersey Police Chiefs' Association gives a big one. Some years, a group of boss fishmongers in Fulton Market gives a big one. Some years, the Palisades Interstate Park Commission gives a big one. The biggest on the river is one that

Harry and Mrs. Lyons have been giving for over twenty years for the benefit of the building fund of Mrs. Lyons' church. This bake is held on the river-bank a short distance above the George Washington Bridge, usually on the Sunday following Mother's Day Sunday, and every year around two hundred and fifty people come to it.

Mrs. Lyons is a handsome, soft-spoken blond woman, quite a few years younger than Harry. She is a native of Fort Lee, the next town on the river north of Edgewater. Her maiden name was Kotze, her parents were Swiss-German, and she was brought up a Roman Catholic. When she was a young woman, out of curiosity, while visiting a friend in Brooklyn, she attended a meeting of a congregation of the Reorganized Church of Jesus Christ of Latter Day Saints, which is the oldest and most widespread of several schismatic branches of the Mormon religion. A number of prophecies and warnings from the Book of Mormon, an apocalyptic Mormon scripture, were read at the meeting, and she was deeply impressed by them. She borrowed a copy of the Book and studied it for some weeks, whereupon she left the Catholic Church and joined the Reorganized Church. The congregation with which she is affiliated holds its services in a hall in the Masonic Temple in Lyndhurst, New Jersey. Harry was brought up an Episcopalian, but he doesn't feel strongly about denominations—

one is as good as another to him—and since his marriage he has gone regularly to the Reorganized
Church services. Harry and his wife have one daughter, Audrey. She is a member of the Reorganized
Church, and went to Graceland College, a junior college sponsored by the church, in Lamoni, Iowa. She
is married to John Maxcy, who is a Buick salesman in
Englewood, New Jersey, and they have two children—Michele, who is sixteen, and Brian, who is
eleven.

Harry is generally supposed to know more about
the river than any of the other rivermen, and a great
deal of what he knows was handed down to him; his
family has lived beside the river for a long time, and
many of his ancestors on both sides were rivermen.
He has old Dutch blood and old English blood, and
gravestones of ancestors of his are all over the
Edgewater Cemetery. He is related to several of the
oldest families in New York and New Jersey. Through
his mother, who was a Truax, he is a descendant of
Philippe du Trieux, one of the first settlers of New
York City. Du Trieux was a Walloon who lived in
Amsterdam and who came to New Amsterdam in
1624 and built a house either on a lane that is now
Beaver Street or on a lane that is now Pearl Street—
the historians aren't sure which. A scholarly study of
his descendants—the name has been spelled Truex
or Truax for generations—was published in install-

ments in *The New York Genealogical and Biographical Record* in 1926, 1927, and 1928. In this study, Harry is listed in the tenth generation of descent from du Trieux.

Harry was born in the upper part of Edgewater, in May, 1884. The house in which he was born is still standing; it is just up the street from the house he lives in now. He went to school in what people of his generation in Edgewater refer to as "the old schoolhouse." This was a wooden building on River Road, on a bluff above the river. It had only two rooms—one for the lower grades and one for the upper grades—and was torn down many years ago. I once heard several old-timers sitting around the barge stove in Ingold's garage get on the subject of the old schoolhouse. One of them, former Fire Chief Lasher, said that he had gone to it, and mentioned a number of men around town who had gone to it at the same time, among them Bill Ingold and Charlie Allison and Harry Lyons, and I asked him what kind of student Harry Lyons had been. "Oh, Harry was bright enough, but he was like the rest of us—he didn't apply himself," Chief Lasher said. "All he studied was the river. At recess, he'd race down to the river and fool around in the mud and attend to some old eelpot he had down there, or crab trap, or bait car, or whatever it was, and I've never in my life seen anybody get so muddy. He was famous for it.

He'd get that sticky river mud all over him, and he wouldn't even try to get it off. Some days, when recess was over, he'd be so muddy the teacher wouldn't let him come back in—she'd send him home. I've been watching rivermen a long time, and they're all like that; they love the mud. Harry's nickname was Hotch. People in Edgewater used to have an expression, if they wanted to say that somebody or something was unusually muddy, they'd say that he or she or it was as muddy as Hotch Lyons. Once in a long while, you still hear somebody come out with that expression. I was standing in line in the A. & P. one day last summer and just ahead of me were two ladies my age. I went to school with them, and I remember them when they were little girls, and I remember them when they were young women, and I remember them when they were middle-aged women in the prime of life, and I imagine the same thought that crosses my mind when I look at them nowadays must also cross their minds when they look at me—How fast time flew! So we were standing there, and one of them turned to the other and said, 'The rain this morning beat down my tomato bushes, and I went out and tried to straighten them up, and I got as muddy as Hotch Lyons,' and all three of us burst out laughing. It brought back the old times."

Harry's father, William Masters Lyons, was an engineer on the Edgewater ferry. Harry was never as close to him as he was to his maternal grandfather, Isaac Truax, who was a riverman. "My father had a good disposition, but he was serious," Harry says. "My grandfather Truax would say things that were funny—at least, to me. He would mimic people and say awful things about them. When I was just a little tiny boy, I began to eat most of my meals at his house and follow him around. He was a great one for going out on the river in the wind and the rain and all kinds of weather, and I'd go along. And then, on a nice sunshiny day, when he should've been out on the river, he'd sit on the porch and read. He didn't have much education, and he didn't even think much of schools, but he had three books that he liked—two books of Shakespeare's writings that had come down to him from his father, and a big Bible with pictures in it that would lift the hair on your head—and he'd sometimes read things to me and explain them, or try to."

Mr. Truax shadfished, and set fykes. A fyke is a long, tunnel-like net that is set on or close to the bottom. It is held open by a series of wooden hoops; a pair of wings flaring out from its mouth guide fish into it; and it catches a little of everything. The spring when Harry was fifteen, Mr. Truax made an unusually large fyke and set it in an inshore channel of the river, off Fort Lee, and Harry quit school to help him operate it. "I decided it was about time for me to graduate from school," Harry says, "so I graduated out the back door." Once or twice a week, if fish prices were good in the city, Mr. Truax and Harry would empty the fyke and row or sail their catch down to one of the riverfront markets in lower Manhattan. Sometimes they would go to Gansevoort Market or Washington Market, on the Hudson, and sometimes they would keep on and go around the Battery to Fulton Market, on the East River. Mr. Truax owned a horse and wagon. If prices were poor, he and Harry would drive out in the country and sell their fish at farmhouses. "My grandfather knew all the fish-eating country people in this part of Bergen County," Harry says, "and they liked to see him coming down the road. If they didn't have any money to spend he'd swap them fish for anything they had, and we'd go home with a wide variety of country produce in the wagon—sausage meat and head-cheese and blood pudding and hard cider and buttermilk and duck eggs and those good old heavy yellow-fleshed strong turnipy-tasting turnips that they call rutabagas, and stuff like that. One day, we drove up in a man's yard, and he had just cut down a bee tree in the woods in back of his house, and we swapped him a bucket of live eels for a quart of wild honey."

When Harry was nineteen, Mr. Truax gave up fishing with fykes and began to depend entirely on what he made from shadfishing. For ten years or so,

Harry helped him fish a couple of rows of shad nets in the spring, and worked the rest of the year at jobs he picked up on or around the river. He worked mostly as a deckhand on tugboats. He worked on two of the Valvoline Oil Company's tugs, the *Magnet* and the *Magic Safety,* and on several of the tugs in the New York, New Haven & Hartford's fleet. Mr. Truax died in 1913, aged eighty-four. For three years thereafter, Harry fished a row of shad nets of his own and set a fyke of his own. In 1915, he got married, and began to worry about money for the first time in his life. In 1916, a fireman's job became open in the Edgewater Fire Department, and he took it. Edgewater has three firehouses. Firehouse No. 1, in which Harry was stationed, is on River Road, a few yards north of the site of the old schoolhouse. It faces the river, and it has a wooden bench in front of it. "Before I joined the Fire Department," Harry once said, "my main occupation was sitting down looking at the river. After I joined the department, that continued to be my main occupation, only I got paid for it." He was a fireman for twenty-six years, and was allowed to take a leave of absence every spring and fish a row of shad nets. He became eligible for a pension in 1942. On April 1st of that year, at the start of the shad season, he retired, and resumed his life as a full-time riverman.

In the spring, Harry sets shad nets. In the fall, he

sets eelpots. Some days, he goes crabbing. Now and then, in every season, not for money but for fun and for the table, he fishes with a hand line or a bamboo pole or a rod and reel. He is an accomplished bait-caster, and it is a pleasure to watch him stand on the bank and cast a knot of bloodworms to the outer edge of the flats, out past the wrecks, and bring in a striped bass. He isn't a striped-bass snob, however, and he often joins the old men and women who come down to the river on sunny afternoons and pole-fish from the bank for anything at all that will bite. Many of the old men and women are opinionated and idio-syncratic, and he enjoys listening to them, and observing the odd rigs that they devise and the imagi-native baits that they use. Around Edgewater, catfish and tomcod and lafayettes and eels are about the only fish that can be caught close to the bank, but that is all right with Harry; he doesn't look down on any of these fish. In common with most of the rivermen, he has a great liking for catfish; he likes to catch them and he likes to eat them. In the spring and early sum-mer, large numbers of catfish show up in the lower Hudson; the spring freshets bring them down from fresh water. Some are enormous. In 1953, one was caught near the George Washington Bridge that weighed over thirty pounds, and every year a few are caught around Edgewater that weigh between ten and twenty pounds. One Saturday afternoon last spring, an old Negro woman fishing a short distance up the bank from Harry caught two big ones, one right after the other. Harry and several other fishermen went over to look at them, and one of the fishermen, who had a hand scale, weighed them; the first weighed seventeen pounds and the second weighed twelve. Harry asked the old woman what kind of bait she had been using. "Chicken guts," she said. Harry also has a great liking for tomcod. The tomcod is a greedy little inshore fish that belongs to the cod family and resembles the deep-sea codfish in every respect but size—it seldom gets much longer than seven inches or weighs more than half a pound, and it gives the appearance of being a midget codfish. It comes into the waters around the city to feed and to spawn, and it is almost as ubiquitous as the eel. There are a few tomcod in every part of the harbor every month of the year. In the late fall and early winter, during their spawning runs, they are abundant, and some days thousands upon thousands of them are caught from piers and sea walls and bulkheads and jetties all the way from Rockaway Point to the Battery, and from the banks of the Hudson and the East River and the Harlem River and the Arthur Kill and the Kill van Kull. They are eaten mainly in the homes of the people who catch them; I have rarely seen them in fish stores, and have never seen them on a menu. Harry thinks the tomcod is greatly undervalued; it is what he calls a sweet-meated fish, and he considers it the best fish, next to shad and snapper bluefish, that enters the river. "There's only one thing wrong with tommycods," he once said. "It takes seventeen of them to make a dozen." On sunny, crystal-clear mornings in the fall, when it is possible to see into the water, he gets in one of his boats and rows out into the flats and catches some river shrimp. River shrimp—they are also called harbor shrimp and mud shrimp, and are really prawns—are tiny; they are only about an inch and a quarter long, including the head. There are sometimes dense swarms of them in the slues between the barges. Harry catches them with a dip net and empties them into a bucket. When he has a supply, he rows farther out into the flats and ties up to one of the old wrecks and sits there and fishes for tomcod, using a hand line and baiting the hook with the shrimp. Occasionally, he pops some of the shrimp into his mouth—he eats them raw and spits out the shells. By noon, as a rule, he has all the tomcod he can use; he has often caught a hundred and fifty in a morning.

Every so often during January, February, and March, Harry gets up early and puts some sand-wiches in his pockets and goes down to his barge and starts a fire in one of the stoves in it and spends the day working on his shadfishing gear. While the river wind hisses and purrs and pipes and whistles through cracks and knotholes in the sides of the barge, he paints an anchor, or overhauls an outboard motor, or makes one net out of the strongest parts of two or three old ones. He works in a leisurely fashion, and keeps a pot of coffee on the stove. Sometimes he goes over and sits beside a window and watches the traffic on the river for an hour or so. Quite often, in the afternoon, one of the other rivermen comes in and helps himself to a cup of coffee and sits down and gossips for a while. Harry's barge is a big one. It is a hundred and ten feet long and thirty-two feet wide. Except for narrow little decks at its bow and stern, it is covered with a superstructure made of heart-pine posts and white-pine clapboards. The superstructure is patched here and there with tar paper, and has a tar-paper roof. It is an old Delaware, Lackawanna & Western barge; on its sides are faded signs that say, "D L & W # 530." It is forty-two years old. When it was thirty years old, a fire that broke out in some cargo damaged parts of its interior; the Lackawanna repaired it and used it for two more years, and then sold it to Harry. Harry has partitioned off two rooms in the bow end of it—one for a galley and one for a bunkroom. In the middle of the bunkroom is a statuesque old claw-footed Sam Oak stove. Around the stove are seven rickety chairs, no two of which are mates. One is a swivel chair whose spring has collapsed. Built against one of the partitions, in three tiers, are twelve bunks. Harry usually makes a fire in the Sam Oak stove and works in the bunkroom; there is a stove in the galley that burns bottled gas and is much easier to manage, but he feels more at home with the Sam Oak, which burns coal or wood. He sometimes uses driftwood that he picks up on the riverbank. The galley and the bunkroom take up less than a third of the space in the barge. The rest of the space is used for storage, and scattered about in it are oars and sweeps and hawsers and kerosene lanterns and shad-bake planks and tin tubs and blocks and tackles and cans of boat paint and sets of scales and stacks of fish boxes. Hanging in festoons from the rafters are dozens of nets, some of which are far too old and ripped and rotten ever to be put in the water again.

One day in late February, the weather was surprisingly sunny and warm. It was one of those balmy days that sometimes turn up in the winter, like a strange bird blown off its course. Walking back to my office after lunch, I began to dawdle. Suddenly the idea occurred to me, why not take the afternoon off and go over to Edgewater and go for a walk along the river and breathe a little clean air for a change. I fought a brief fight with my conscience, and then I entered the Independent subway at Forty-second Street and rode up to the 168th Street station and went upstairs to the Public Service bus terminal and got a No. 8 bus. This bus goes across the George Washington Bridge and heads south and runs through a succession of riverfront towns, the second of which is Edgewater. It is a pleasant trip in itself. At the town limits of Edgewater, there is a sign that says, "WELCOME TO EDGEWATER. WHERE HOMES AND INDUSTRY BLEND. EDGEWATER CHAMBER OF COMMERCE." A couple of bus stops past this sign, I got out, as I usually do, and began to walk along River Road. I looked at my watch; I had made good connections, and the trip from Forty-second Street had taken only thirty-six minutes. The sunshine was so warm that my overcoat felt burdensome. All along the west side of River Road, women had come out into their front yards and were slowly walking around, looking at the dead stalks and vines in their flower beds. I saw a woman squat sideways beside what must have been a bulb border and rake away some leaves with her fingers. She peered at the ground for a few moments, and then swept the leaves back with one sweep of her hand. In the upper part of Edgewater, River Road is high above the river, and a steep, wooded slope lies between the east side of it and the riverbank. Just past the George Washington School, a public school on the site of the old schoolhouse, there is a bend in the road from which it is possible to look down almost on the tops of the shad barges drawn up close to the riverbank along there. I looked the barges over, and picked out Harry's. Smoke was coming from its stovepipe, and I decided to stop by and have a cup of coffee with Harry. Several paths descend from the road to the riverbank. Children like to slide on them and play on them, and they are deeply rutted. As I started down one of them, Harry came out on the bow deck of his barge and looked up and saw me and waved. A few minutes later, I crossed the riverbank and went out on the ramshackle footwalk that extends from the riverbank to his barge and climbed the ladder that is fixed to the bow and stepped on deck, and he and I shook hands. "Go inside and get yourself a cup of coffee and bring it out here, why don't you," he said, "and let's sit in the sun a little while."

When I returned to the deck, Harry motioned toward the riverbank with his head and said, "Look who's coming." Two men had just started up the footwalk. One was a stranger to me. The other was an old friend and contemporary of Harry's named Joe Hewitt. I have run into him a number of times, and have got to know him fairly well. Mr. Hewitt is six feet two and portly and red-faced. He lives in Fort Lee, but he is a native of Edgewater and belongs to one of the old Edgewater families. He went to school in the old schoolhouse at the same time as Harry, and fished and worked around the river for a few years, and then went to a business school on Park Row, in Manhattan, called the City Hall Academy. Through an uncle, who was in the trucking business and often trucked shad from Edgewater and other riverfront towns to Fulton Market during the shad season, he got a job as a clerk in the old Fulton Market firm of John Feeney, Inc. He became head bookkeeper in Feeney's, and subsequently worked for several other firms in the fish market. He retired over ten years ago. He spends a lot of time in Edgewater, and often hangs out in Ingold's garage. Years ago, Mr. Hewitt bought three tracts of cheap land along the Hackensack River, one in Hudson County and two in Bergen County; he speaks of them as "those mosquito bogs of mine." In recent years, two of these tracts have increased in value enormously, and he has sold sections of them for housing developments and shopping centers, and has become well-to-do. He is a generous man, and often goes out of his way to help people. Once in a while, a riverman gets in a bad jam of some kind and is broke to begin with and other rivermen take up a collection for him, and Mr. Hewitt almost always gives more than anyone else. However, despite his generosity and kindness, he has a bleak outlook on life, and doesn't try to hide it. "Things have worked out very well for you, Joe," I once heard another retired man remark to him one day in Ingold's garage, "and you ought to look at things a little more cheerful than you do." "I'm not so sure I have anything to be cheerful about," Mr. Hewitt replied. "I'm not so sure you have, either. I'm not so sure anybody has."

"Who is the man with Mr. Hewitt?" I asked Harry.

"I never saw him before," Harry said.

Mr. Hewitt came up the ladder first, and stepped on deck, puffing and blowing.

"The sun was so nice we decided to walk down from Fort Lee," he said, "and what a mistake that was! The traffic is getting worse and worse on River Road. Oh, it scares me! Those big heavy trucks flying past, it's worth your life to step off the curb. Slam on their brakes, they couldn't stop; you'd be in the hospital before they even slowed down. You'd be lying on the operating table with an arm off, an arm and a leg, an arm and a leg and one side of your head, and they'd still be rolling. And the noise they make! The shot and shell on the battlefield wouldn't be much worse. What was that old poem? How'd it go, how'd it go? I used to know it. 'In Flanders fields the poppies blow, between the crosses, row on row . . .' And good God, gentlemen, the Cadillacs! While we were standing there, waiting and waiting for a chance to cross, six big black Cadillacs shot by, practically one right after the other, and it wasn't any funeral, either."

"Times are good, Joe," said Harry. "Times are good."

"Thieves," said Mr. Hewitt.

His companion reached the top of the ladder and awkwardly stepped on deck. "Gentlemen," said Mr. Hewitt, "this is my brother-in-law Frank Townsend." He turned to Harry. "Harry," he said, "you've heard me speak of Frank. He's Blanche's younger brother, the one who's in the sprinkler-system business. Or was. He's retired now." He turned to me. "Blanche is my wife," he said. Then he turned to Mr. Townsend. "Sit down, Frank," he said, "and get your breath." Mr. Townsend sat down on a capstan. "Frank lives in Syracuse," continued Mr. Hewitt. "He's been down in Florida, and he's driving back, and he's spending a few days with us. Since he retired, he's got interested in fishing. I told him the shadfishermen all along the Hudson are getting ready for shad season, and he's never seen a shad barge, and I thought I'd bring him down here and show him one, and explain shadfishing to him."

Harry's eyebrows rose. "Shadfishing hasn't changed much through the years, Joe," he said, "but it's been a long, long time since you lifted a net. Maybe you better let me do the explaining."

"I wish you would," said Mr. Hewitt. "I was hoping you would."

"I'll make it as brief as possible," said Harry,

walking over to the edge of the deck. "Step over here, Mr. Townsend, and look over the side. Do you see those poles lying down there in the mud? They're shagbark-hickory poles, and they're fifty to seventy feet long, and they're the foundation of shadfishing; everything else depends on them. During shad season, we stick them up in the river in rows at right angles to the shore, and hitch our nets to them. When the season's finished, we pull them up and bring them in here in the flats and bed them in the mud on both sides of our barges until we're ready to use them again. They turn green down there, from the green slime, but that's all right—the slime preserves them. As long as we keep them damp, they stay strong and supple and sound. If we let them dry out, they lose their strength and their give and start to rot."

Mr. Townsend interrupted Harry. "How much do they cost you?" he asked.

"Shad is an expensive fish, Mr. Townsend, not to speak of shad roe," Harry said, "and one of the reasons is it's expensive to fish for. You can't just pick up the phone and order a shad pole from a lumberyard. You have to hunt all over everywhere and find a farmer who has some full-grown hickory trees in his woods and is willing to sell some, and even then he might not have any that are tall enough and straight enough and strong enough and limber enough. I get mine from a farmer who owns some deep woods in Pennsylvania. When I need some new ones, I go out there—in the dead of winter, usually, a couple of months before shad season starts—and spend the whole day tramping around in his woods looking at his hickories. And I don't just look at a tree—I study it from all sides and try to imagine how it would take the strain if it was one of a row of poles staked in the Hudson River holding up a shad net and the net was already heavy with fish and a full-moon tide was pushing against the net and bellying it out and adding more fish to it all the time. I study hundreds of them. Then I pick out the likeliest-looking ones and blaze them with an axe. The farmer cuts them down, and sends them up here on a trailer truck. Then I and a couple of men around the river go to work on them and peel their bark off and trim their knots off and smooth them down with adzes and drawknives and planes until there's no splinters or rough spots on them anywhere that the net could catch on. Then we sharpen their butt ends, to make it easier to drive them into the river bottom. I pay the farmer eighteen to twenty dollars apiece for them. After the trucking charges are added to that, and the wages of the men who help me trim them, I figure they cost me between thirty-five and forty dollars apiece. You need at least forty of them for every row you fish. Tugboats are always blundering into them at night and passing right over them and bending them down until they crack in two, so you also have to have a supply of spares set aside. In other words, the damned things run into money."

Some young girls—there were perhaps a dozen of them, and they were eight or nine or maybe ten years old—had come down one of the paths from River Road, and now they were chasing each other around on the riverbank. They were as overexcited as blue jays, and their fierce, jubilant, fresh young voices filled the air.

"School's out," said Harry.

Several of the girls took up a position near the shore end of the footwalk to Harry's barge. Two of them started turning a rope and singing a rope-jumping song, a third ran in and started jumping the rope, and the others got in line. The song began:

> *Mama, Mama,*
> *I am ill.*
> *Send for the doctor*
> *To give me a pill.*
> *Doctor, Doctor,*
> *Will I die?*
> *Yes, my child,*
> *And so will I—*

Mr. Hewitt looked at them gloomily. "They get louder every year," he said.

"I like to hear them," said Harry. "It's been sixty years since I was in school, but I know exactly how they feel. Now, Mr. Townsend, to get back to shad-fishing," he continued, "the first thing a man starting out as a shadfisherman has to have is a supply of poles, and the next thing he has to have is a row—that is, a place in the river where he can stake his poles year after year. In the old days, a man could pretty much decide for himself where his row should be, just so he didn't get too close to another man's row or get out in a ship channel or interfere with access to a pier. However, the shipping interests and the tugboat interests were always complaining that the shadfishermen acted as if they owned the river, and vice versa, so the Army Engineers finally stepped in. The Engineers have jurisdiction over all the navigable rivers in the country, insofar as the protection of navigation is concerned. About twenty years ago, just before World War Two, they went out and made a study of the Hudson from the standpoint of shad-fishing versus navigation, and the outcome was they abolished some of the rows and left some right where they were and moved some and laid out a few new ones. Every year, they re-survey the rows, and some years they move or abolish one or two more. The best rows are in what's called the lower river—the section from the mouth of the river, down at the Battery, to the east-and-west boundary line between

New Jersey and New York, which is about twenty miles up. Now, all the way up to this point the north-and-south boundary line between the two states is the middle of the river, and it so happens that all this distance all the shad rows are in the half of the river that belongs to New Jersey—there can't be any over in the New York half, because the main ship channel is in it. At present, there are fifty-five of these rows. The first row is off the big New York Central grain elevator in the railroad yards in Weehawken, about on a level with Sixtieth Street in Manhattan. It's a short row, only five hundred feet across, and it's entirely too near the ocean-liner traffic to suit me. Now and then, a big Cunarder or a Furness Line boat or a Swedish American Line boat will back out of one of the piers in the Fifties, and when she gets out in the river she'll keep on backing to get in position to go down the channel, and her backwash will hit the first row and churn the net up and down and whip it against the poles and empty the fish out of it. Some days, the backwash of those boats can be felt practically all the way to Albany. The fifty-fifth row is off the village of Alpine, which is about on a level with Yonkers and just below the east-and-west boundary line. Up above this line, the whole river belongs to New York, and the New York shadfishermen take over. Some of them fish the same as we do, in rows, with nets hitched to poles, but most of them fish with nets that they drift from boats. Their rows aren't as good as ours. One reason is, you're bound to catch more fish if you have the first crack at them. And another reason is, the sooner shad are caught after they leave the sea—or, a plainer way of putting it, the less time they spend in the river water—the better they taste and the more they're worth. The Engineers have the say-so as to where a row can be placed, but the Conservation Department of the state in whose waters the row is located has the say-so as to who can fish it. The New Jersey rows don't change hands very often; once a man gets one, he can renew his rights to it every year, and he generally holds on to it until he dies, and then it goes to whoever's next on the waiting list. You don't rent a row—what you do is, every year you take out a license for each row you fish, and a license costs twenty-five dollars. Most of the rows off Edgewater and Weehawken are very old. One of the Edgewater rows has been fished for at least a hundred and fifty years, and maybe a good while longer. A man named Bill Ingold fishes it now, but it's still called the Truax row, after my grandfather, Isaac Truax, who fished it for many years. When my grandfather had it, it was called the Scott row, after the man who had it ahead of him. I've heard the name of the man who had it ahead of Scott and the name of the man who had it ahead of him, but they've faded out of my mind. I've got two rows in my name. They're the first two rows north of the George Washington Bridge. They're both twelve-hundred-foot rows, which is the length of most of the rows. The last few years, I've been fishing only one of them the whole season through. It's the lower one. If you ever drive over the bridge on the west-bound roadway during shad season, look up the river a little ways and you'll see my poles."

Mr. Townsend had grown tired of standing, and he sat back down on the capstan.

"Sometime in the latter half of March," continued Harry, "I and three or four men that I swap labor with get together and move this barge up the river. They help me move mine, I help them move theirs; they help me stake my poles, I help them stake theirs. We tie the barge to a launch owned by one of the men and tow her up on the tide, and take her to a point beside the riverbank half a mile or so above the bridge, where she'll be convenient to both my rows. We run a hawser from that capstan you're sitting on to a tree on the bank and draw her up close to the bank, with the bow facing the bank, and then we anchor her with three anchors—port, starboard, and stern. She stays there for the duration of shad season. Then we get out on the bank and put up a rack to mend nets on and a gallows to hang a set of scales on. The land along there is owned by the Palisades Interstate Park, and a shadfisherman pays rent for the space he uses on the riverbank on the basis of how many rows he fishes—the rate is two hundred dollars a row for the season. Then we go back to the flats and start snaking my poles out of the mud and loading them on a peculiar-looking kind of craft called a double boat. A double boat consists of two forty-foot scows connected together side by side but with a narrow space left in between them. It resembles a raft, as much as it resembles anything. When we get it loaded, we tow it up the river on the tide, the same as we towed the barge, and then we start staking the poles. Until a few years ago, this was a job shadfishermen dreaded. We'd anchor the double boat over the place we wanted the pole to go, and we'd stand the pole up in the narrow in-between space I mentioned, to keep it steady. Then we'd lash a crosspiece on the pole, and two men, the heavier the better, would climb up and stand on the crosspiece and hold on to the pole and bend their knees and make a kind of jumping motion, keeping time with each other, until they drove the butt end of the pole into the river bottom. Sometimes they'd have to jump for hours to get a pole down far enough. Sometimes more weight would be needed and two more men would get up on the crosspiece. The two on the inside would hold on to the pole and the two on the outside would hold on to the two on the inside, and they'd jump and grunt and jump and grunt, and it was a strange sight to watch, particularly to people watching it from shore who didn't have the slightest idea what was going on out there. Shad poles are spaced from twenty-five to thirty feet apart, and you have to put down from forty-one to forty-nine poles on a twelve-hundred-foot row, counting the outside poles, so you can just imagine the jumping we used to have to do. Nowadays, it's much simpler. We have a winch sitting on a platform in the middle of the double boat, and we simply stand the pole in place and put a short length of chain around it up toward its upper end and hook a cable from the winch onto the chain, and the winch exerts a powerful downward pull on the chain and forces the butt end of the pole into the bottom.

"By the last week in March, the shad barges are in place all along the Hudson and the shad poles are up. There's a number of old retired or half-retired sea cooks and tugboat cooks in Edgewater and Weehawken, and they come out of retirement around this time and take jobs as cooks on shad barges. They work on the same barges year after year. As soon as the cooks get situated in the galleys, the shadfishermen start living aboard. Around the same time, men start showing up in Edgewater who haven't been seen in town since last shad season. You need highly skilled fishermen to handle shad nets, and for many years there hasn't been enough local help to go around, so every spring fishermen from other places come and take the jobs. A shadfisherman generally hires from two to five of them for each row he fishes, and pays them a hundred or so a week and bunk and board. Most of them are Norwegians or Swedes. Some come from little ports down in South Jersey, such as Atlantic Highlands, Port Monmouth, Keyport, Point Pleasant, and Wildwood. In other seasons, they do lobstering or pound-fishing, or go out on draggers or scallopers. Some come from a small dragger fleet that works out of Mill Basin, in Brooklyn. Some come from Fulton Market—old fishermen who work as fillet cutters and go back to fishing only during shad season. Some don't come from any particular place, but roam all over. One man didn't show up in Edgewater year before last, the best man with a shad net I ever saw, and last year he did show up, and I asked him where he'd been. 'I worked my way home on a tanker to see my sister,' he said, and by 'home' he meant some port in Norway, 'and then I worked on a Norwegian sealer that hunted harp seals along the coast of Labrador, and then I worked my way back here on a tanker, and then I worked awhile in the shrimp fleet in Galveston, Texas, and the last few months I worked on a bait-clam dredge in Sheepshead Bay.' They know how to do almost any kind of commercial fishing— and if they don't they can pick it up between breakfast and lunch and do it better by supper than the ones who taught them. When they come aboard a barge, all they ever have with them is an old suitcase in one hand and an old sea bag slung over one shoulder that they carry their boots and oilskins in, and they seldom say much about themselves. In times past, there were quite a few rummies among them, real old thirty-second-degree rummies, but the rummies seem to have dropped by the wayside. Oh, there's a few left.

"Every year, on one of the last days in March or one of the first days in April, the shad start coming in from the sea. They enter the mouth of the harbor, at Sandy Hook, and straggle around awhile in the Lower Bay, and then they go through the Narrows and cross the Upper Bay and enter the mouth of the Hudson and head for their spawning grounds. There are several of these grounds. The main one begins eighty miles up the river, up around Kingston, and extends to Coxsackie—a distance of twenty-five miles. This stretch of the river has a great many sandbars in it, and creek mouths and shallow coves and bays. As a rule, shad are four years old when they make their first trip in, and they keep on coming in once every year until their number is up. You can take a scale off a shad and look at the scars on it and tell how many times the shad has spawned, and every season we see quite a few who managed to escape our nets as many as five or six times and go up and spawn before they finally got caught, not to speak of the fact that they managed to keep from being eaten by some other fish all those years. Roe shad average around three and a half to four pounds, and bucks average around two and a half to three. The roes are always heavier. Once in a while, we see a seven-pound roe, or an eight-pounder, or a nine-pounder. I caught one once that weighted thirteen and a half pounds."

"Just think how many fish she must've spawned in her time," said Mr. Townsend. "If it had been me that caught her, I'd've patted her on the back and put her back in."

"A commercial fisherman is supposed to catch fish, Mr. Townsend, not put them back in," Harry said. "Anyway, as a matter of fact, I killed her getting her loose from the net. The shad won't come into the river until the temperature of the river water reaches forty degrees or thereabouts, and that's what we watch for. Day after day, when the water starts approaching this temperature, we go out just before every flood tide and hang a short net called a jitney in the spaces between several poles toward the far end of the row. This is a trial net. The shad may start trickling in, only three or four showing up on each tide, and continue that way for days, or avalanches of them may start coming in all at once, but as soon as we find the first ones in the trial net, however many there are, even if there's only one, we go to work in earnest. Just before the next flood tide begins, I and two or three of the hired fishermen take a regular-sized net out to the row in a shad boat. A shad boat is fifteen to twenty feet long and high and sharp in the bow and low and square and roomy in the stern. It has a well in its bottom, up forward, in which to sit an outboard motor—although you can row it if you want to—and it's unusually maneuverable. We have the net piled up in the stern, and we work our way across the downriver side of the row, and go from pole to pole, feeding the net out and letting the bottom of it sink and tying the top of it to the poles. It's like putting up a fence, only it's an underwater fence. Where my row is, the water ranges in depth from twenty to thirty feet, and I use a net that's twenty feet deep. The net has iron rings sewed every few feet along the bottom of it to weight it down and hold it down. In addition, on each end of it, to anchor it, we tie a stone called a dropstone. Several blocks north of here, there's a ravine running down from River Road to the riverbank. In the middle of the ravine is a brook, and beside the brook is an old abandoned wagon road all grown over with willow trees and sumac and sassafras and honeysuckle and poison ivy. Years ago, the main business of Edgewater was cutting paving blocks for New York City, and wagons carrying loads of these blocks to a dock on the riverbank used to come down this road. It was a rocky road, and you can still see ruts that the wheel rims wore in the rocks. Through the years, a good many paving blocks bounced off the wagons and fell in the brook, and the drivers were too lazy to pick them up, and that's where we get our dropstones. If we lose one in the river, we go up with a crowbar and root around in the mud and tree roots and rusty tin cans in the bed of the brook and dig out another one. Some of us have a notion the blocks are lucky. I wouldn't think of using any other kind of dropstone.

"By the time we have the net hung all the way across, the flood tide is in full flow, pushing and pressing against the net and bellying it out in the spaces between the poles. We go on back to the barge and leave the net to take care of itself for the duration of the tide. If enough shad to amount to anything come up the river in the tide, some of them are bound to hit it. They'll either hit it head on and stick their heads in the meshes and gill themselves or they'll hit it sideways and tangle themselves in it and the tide will hold them against it the way the wind holds a scrap of paper against a fence. In this part of the river, the tide runs from three and a half to six hours, according to the time of the month and the strength and direction of the wind, and it runs faster on the bottom than it does on the top, and it'll trick you. When we judge it's getting on toward the time it should start slowing down, we go back out to the row in the shad boat and get ready to lift the net. Quite often, we're way too early, and have to stop at the first pole and sit there in the boat with our hands in our laps and bide our time. We might sit there an hour. If it's during the day, we sit and look up at the face of the Palisades, or we look at the New York Central freight trains that seem to be fifteen miles long streaking by on the New York side, or we look downriver at the tops of the skyscrapers in the distance. I've never been able to make up my mind about the New York skyline. Sometimes I think it's beautiful, and sometimes I think it's a gaudy damned unnatural sight. If it's in the nighttime, we look at that queer glare over midtown Manhattan that comes from the lights in Times Square. On cold, clear nights in April, sitting out on the river in the dark, that glare in the sky looks like the Last Judgment is on the way, or the Second Coming, or the end of the world. Every little while, we stick an oar straight into the water and try to hold it there, to test the strength of the tide. We have to time things very carefully. We want the net to stay down and catch fish as long as possible, but if we wait too long to get started the tide will begin to ebb before we get across the row, and belly the net in the opposite direction, and dump the fish out. I sit beside the outboard motor and handle the boat, and I usually have three fishermen

aboard. When I give the signal to let's get going, two
of the fishermen stand up side by side in the stern,
and one unties the net at the first pole. Then, while
one holds on to the top of the net, the other pulls the
bottom of it up to the top—that's called pursing it.
Then they start drawing it into the boat, a little at a
time. The third man stands a few feet farther back,
and helps wherever he's needed most. We proceed
from pole to pole, untying the net and drawing it in.
As it comes aboard, the men shake it and jerk it and
twitch it and seesaw it and yank it this way and that,
and the fish spill out of it and fall to the bottom of
the boat. The men tear a lot of holes in the net that
way, but it can't be helped. As the net piles up in the
stern, the fish pile up amidships. When we get to the
end of the row, if we've had a good lift, we'll have
over a thousand shad piled up amidships, bucks and
roes all jumbled together, flipping and flopping and
beating the air with their tails, each and every one of
them fit to be cooked by some great chef at the
Waldorf-Astoria and served on the finest china, and
the boat'll almost be awash. I must've seen a million
shad in my time, and I still think they're beautiful—
their thick bodies, their green backs, their silver
sides, their saw-edged bellies, the deep forks in their
tails. The moment we draw in the end of the net, we
turn about and head for the riverbank. We beach the
boat, and all four of us grab hold of the net—it's

dripping wet and heavy as lead—and heave it onto a kind of low-sided box with four handles on it called a net box. We carry this up on the bank, and spread the net on the net rack. Then, while one man starts picking river trash out of the net and mending it and getting it ready for the next flood tide, I and the two other men unload the fish and sort them and weigh them and pack them in wooden boxes, a hundred or so pounds to a box. The roes bring a much higher price than the bucks, and we pack them separately. I write my name on each box with a black crayon, and below it I write 'A. & S.' That stands for Ackerly & Sandiford, the wholesale firm in Fulton Market that I ship to. There's always some trucker over here who understands shadfishing and makes a business every spring of trucking shad to market. Joe's uncle, old Mr. John Hewitt, used to do it years ago, first with a dray, then with a truck. In recent years, a man named George Indahl has been doing it. Usually, about the time we get through boxing a lift, one of his trucks comes down the little one-lane dirt road that runs along the riverbank up where I anchor my barge, and the driver stops and picks up my boxes. Then he goes on down the line and stops at the next shadfisher-man's place, and keeps on making stops until he has a load, and then he high-tails it for South Street."

"South Street is the main street in Fulton Market, Frank," Mr. Hewitt said to Mr. Townsend. "Most of the fishmongers have their stands on it. There's an old saying in the market, 'When the shad are running in the Hudson, South Street is bloody.'"

"My place on the riverbank is kind of hard to get to, although you can see it from the bridge," Harry continued, "but the first few days of shad season, every time we come in with a lift, we find a little crowd standing there. They're mostly old men. They stand around and watch us bring the fish ashore and sort them and box them, and the sight of the shad seems to do them good. Some are old men from Edgewater and Fort Lee. Others are old men I never see any other time. They show up year after year, and I say hello to them and shake hands, but I don't know their names, let alone where they come from. I don't even know if they come from New Jersey or New York. Several have been coming for so many years that I tell them to wait until the others have gone, and I give them a shad, a roe shad. They're well-to-do-looking men, some of them, and could probably buy me and sell me, but they bring a newspaper to wrap their fish in and a paper bag to carry it in, and the way they thank me, you'd think I was giving them something really valuable. One of them, who'd been showing up every spring for years and years with his paper bag all neatly folded in his overcoat pocket, didn't show up last spring. 'The poor old boy, whoever he was,' I said to myself, when I happened to think of him, 'he didn't last the winter.' Day by day, the little crowd gets smaller and smaller, and after the first week or so only an occasional person shows up, and things settle down to a routine. Not that they get dull. Lifting a shad net is like shooting dice—you never get tired of seeing what comes up. One lift, we may get only two or three fish all the way across; next lift, we may get a thousand. One lift, we may get mostly bucks; next lift, roes may outnumber bucks three to one. And shad aren't the only fish that turn up in a shad net. We may find a dozen big catfish lying in the belly of the net, or a couple of walleyed pike, or some other kind of fresh-water fish. A freshet brought them down, and they were making their way back up the river, and they hit the net. Or we may find some fish that strayed in from the ocean on a strong tide—bluefish or blackfish or fluke or moss-bunkers or goosefish, or a dozen other kinds. Or we may find some ocean fish that run up the river to spawn the same as shad, such as sea sturgeon or alewives or summer herring. Sea sturgeon are the kind of sturgeon whose roe is made into caviar. Some of them get to be very old and big. Going up the river, they keep leaping out of the water, and suddenly, at least once every season, one of them leaps out of the water right beside my boat, and it's so big and long and ugly and covered all over with warts that it scares me—it might be eight, nine, ten, or eleven feet long and weigh a couple of hundred pounds. We get quite a few of the young ones in our nets, and now and then, especially during the latter part of the season, we lift the net and there's a gaping big hole in it, and we know that a full-grown one came up the river sometime during the tide, an old-timer, and hit the net and went right through it. Several years ago, an eighty-one-pounder hit the net sideways while we were lifting it, and began to plunge around in it, and it was as strong as a young bull, but the men braced themselves and took a firm grip on the net and held on until it wore itself out, and then they pulled it aboard.

"The bulk of the shad go up the river between the middle of April and the middle of May. Around the middle of May, we begin to see large numbers of what we call back-runners coming down the river— shad that've finished spawning and are on their way back to sea. We don't bother them. They eat little or nothing while they're on their spawning runs, and by this time they're so feeble and emaciated they can just barely make it. If we find them in our nets, we shake them back into the water. Shad keep right on coming into the river until around the end of June, but during May the price goes lower and lower, and finally they aren't worth fishing for. In the last week in May or the first week in June, we pull up our poles and move our barges back to the flats.

"The young shad stay up on the spawning grounds through the summer. In October and the early part of November, when the water starts getting cold, they come down the river in huge schools and go out to sea. Way up in November, last year, they were still coming down. One morning, a week or so before Thanksgiving, I was out in the flats, tied up to an old wreck, fishing for tomcod, and all of a sudden the water around my boat became alive with little shad—pretty little silver-sided things, three to five inches in length, flipping right along. I dropped a bucket over the side and brought up half a dozen of them, and they were so lively they made the water in the bucket bubble like seltzer water. I looked at them a few minutes, and then I poured them back in the river. 'Go on out to sea,' I said to them, 'and grow up and get some flesh on your bones, and watch yourselves and don't get eaten by other fish, and four years from now, a short distance above the George Washington Bridge,' I said, 'maybe our paths will cross again.'"

Mr. Townsend and Mr. Hewitt and I had been listening closely to Harry, and none of us had paid any further attention to the young girls jumping rope on the riverbank. Shortly after Harry stopped talking, all of us became aware at the same moment that the girls turning the rope were singing a new song. Just then, the girl jumping missed a jump, and another girl ran in to take her place, whereupon the girls turning the rope started the new song all over again. Their voices were rollicking, and they laughed as they sang. The song began:

> *The worms crawl in,*
> *The worms crawl out.*
> *They eat your guts*
> *And spit them out.*
> *They bring their friends*
> *And their friends' friends, too,*
> *And there's nothing left*
> *When they get through. . . .*

Harry laughed. "They've changed it a little," he said. "That line used to go, 'And you look like hell when they get through.'"

"'The worms crawl in, the worms crawl out. They play pinochle on your snout,'" said Mr. Townsend. "That's the way I remember it. 'One little worm who's not so shy crawls up your nose and out your eye.' That's another line I remember."

"Let's go inside," said Mr. Hewitt. "It's getting cold out here. We'll all catch pneumonia."

"You know what they used to say about pneumonia, Joe," Harry said. " 'Pneumonia is the old man's friend.' "

"A lot of what they used to say," said Mr. Hewitt, "could just as well've been left unsaid."

Stooping, he stepped from the deck into the passageway of the barge and walked past the galley and into the bunkroom, and the rest of us followed. There is a bulletin board on the partition that separates the bunkroom from the storage quarters beyond. Tacked on it are mimeographed notices dating back ten years concerning new shadfishing regulations or changes in old ones—some from the Corps of Engineers, United States Army, and some from the Division of Fish and Game, Department of Conservation and Economic Development, State of New Jersey. Also tacked on the bulletin board is a flattened-out pasteboard box on which someone has lettered with boat paint: "OLD FISHERMEN NEVER DIE—THEY JUST SMELL THAT WAY." Tacked on the partition to the right of the bulletin board are several Coast and Geodetic charts of the river and the harbor. Tacked to the left of it are a number of group photographs taken at shad bakes run by Harry. One photograph shows a group of fishmongers from Fulton Market lined up in two rows at a shad bake on the riverbank, and Mr. Hewitt himself is in the second row. The fishmongers are looking straight at the camera. Several are holding up glasses of beer. All have big smiles on their faces. Mr. Hewitt went over to this photograph and began to study it. Mr. Townsend and I sat down in chairs beside the stove. Harry opened the stove door and punched up the fire with a crowbar. Then he sat down.

"Oh, God, Harry," said Mr. Hewitt after he had studied the photograph awhile, "it was only just a few short years ago this picture was made, and a shocking number of the fellows in it are dead already. Here's poor Jimmy McBarron. Jimmy was only forty-five when he died, and he was getting along so well. He was president of Wallace, Keeney, Lynch, one of the biggest firms in the market, and he had an interest in a shrimp company in Florida. And here's Mr. John Matthews, who was secretary-treasurer of Chesebro Brothers, Robbins & Graham. He was a nice man. A little stiff and formal for the fish market. 'How do you do, Mr. Hewitt?' he used to say to me, when everybody else in the market called me Joe, even the lumpers on the piers. And here's Matt Graham, who was one of the partners in the same firm. A nicer man never lived than Matt Graham. He went to work in the market when he was fifteen years of age, and all he ever knew was fish, and all he ever wanted to know was fish."

"I used to ship to him," said Harry. "I shipped to him when he was with Booth Fisheries, long before he went with Chesebro. I shipped him many a box of shad, and he always treated me fair and square."

Mr. Hewitt continued to stare at the photograph.

"This one's alive," he said. "This one's dead. This one's alive. At least, I haven't heard he's dead. Here's Drew Radel, who was president of the Andrew Radel Oyster Company, planters and distributors of Robbins Island oysters. He died only last year. Sixty-five, the paper said. I had no idea he was that far along. I ran into him the summer before he died, and he looked around fifty. He's one man I can honestly say I never heard a bad word spoken about him. Here's a man who kept books for companies all over the market, the same as I did. He worked for Frank Wilkisson and Eastern Commission and George M. Still and Middleton, Carman and Lockwood & Winant and Caleb Haley and Lester & Toner and Blue Ribbon, and I don't know how many others—a real old-fashioned floating bookkeeper. I ate lunch across from him at the front table in Sloppy Louie's two or three times a week year in and year out, and now I can't even think of his name. Eddie Something-or-Other. He's still alive, last I heard. Retired. Lives in Florida. His wife had money; he never saved a cent. Grows grapefruit, somebody said. If I felt I had to grow something, by God, it wouldn't be grapefruit. This man's alive. So's this man. Dead. Dead. Dead. Three in a row. Alive. Alive. Alive. Dead. Alive. And here's a man, I won't mention his name and I shouldn't tell about this, but a couple of years ago, when I saw in the *New York Times* that he was dead, the thought flashed into my mind, 'I do hope they bury him in Evergreen Cemetery.'"

He turned away from the photograph, and came over and sat down.

"And I'll tell you the reason that particular thought flashed into my mind," he said. "This fellow was the biggest woman chaser in the market, and one of the biggest talkers on the subject I ever heard. When he and I were young men in the market together, he used to tell me about certain of his experiences along that line out in Brooklyn, where he lived. Tell *me*—hell! he told everybody that would listen. At that time, Trommer's Brewery was the finest brewery in Brooklyn. It was at the corner of Bushwick Avenue and Conway Street, and out in front of it was a beer garden. The brewery maintained the beer garden, and it was a showplace. They had tables in the open, and a large restaurant indoors with at least a dozen big potted palms stood up in it. During the summer, they had a German orchestra that played waltz music. And directly across the street from the beer garden was the main gate of Evergreen Cemetery. After a burial, it was customary for the mourners to stop in Trommer's beer garden and drown their sorrow in Trommer's White

Label and rejoice in the fact that it was the man or the woman they'd left out in the cemetery's turn to go, and not theirs. On Sundays, people would take the streetcar out to the cemetery and visit the graves of relatives and friends, and then they'd go over to Trommer's beer garden for sandwiches and beer. Now this fellow I'm talking about, he used to dress up on Sundays and go out to the cemetery and walk up and down the cemetery paths until he found some young widow out there by herself visiting her husband's grave, and she didn't have to be too damned young, and he'd go over and get acquainted with her and sympathize with her, and she'd cry and he'd cry, and then he'd invite her over to Trommer's beer garden, and they'd sit there and have some beers and listen to the music and talk, and one thing would lead to another."

Mr. Hewitt leaned over and opened the stove door and spat on the red-hot coals. "To hear him tell it," he said, "he was hell on widows. He knew just what to say to them."

"Did this gentleman ever get married himself?" asked Mr. Townsend. He sounded indignant.

"He was married twice," said Mr. Hewitt. "A year or two before he died, he divorced his first wife and married a woman half his age."

"I hope some man came up to her in the cemetery when she was visiting his grave and got acquainted with her and sympathized with her," Mr. Townsend said, "and one thing led to another."

Mr. Hewitt had lost interest in this turn of the conversation. "It's highly unlikely she ever visited his grave," he said.

Mr. Townsend shrugged his shoulders. "Ah, well," he said. "In that case."

Mr. Hewitt got up and went over and scrutinized the photograph again. "I look a lot older now than I did when this picture was made," he said, "and there's no denying that." He continued to scrutinize the photograph for a few more minutes, and then returned to his chair.

"When I was young," he said, "I had the idea death was for other people. It would happen to other people but not to me. That is, I couldn't really visualize it happening to me. And if I did allow myself to think that it would happen to me, it was very easy to put the thought out of my mind—if it had to take place, it would take place so far in the distant future it wasn't worth thinking about, let alone worrying about, and then the years flew by, and now it's right on top of me. Any time now, as the fellow said, the train will pull into the station and the trip will be over."

"Ah, well," said Mr. Townsend.

"It seems to me it was only just a few short years ago I was a young man going back and forth to work," said Mr. Hewitt, "and the years flew by, they really flew by, and now I'm an old man, and what I want to know is, what was the purpose of it? I know what's going to take place one of these days, and I can visualize some of the details of it very clearly. There'll be one twenty-five-dollar wreath, or floral design, or whatever they call them now, and there'll be three or maybe four costing between twelve dollars and a half and fifteen dollars, and there'll be maybe a dozen running from five to ten dollars, and I know more or less what the preacher will say, and then they'll take me out to the Edgewater Cemetery and lay me beside my parents and my brothers and sisters and two of my grandparents and one of my great-grandparents, and I'll lie there through all eternity while the Aluminum Company factory goes put-put-put."

Harry laughed, "You make the Aluminum Company factory sound like a motorboat," he said.

"I don't go to funerals any more," said Mr. Townsend. "Funerals breed funerals."

"My grandfather used to like the word 'mitigate,'" Harry said. "He liked the sound of it, and he used it whenever he could. When he was a very old man, he often got on the subject of dying. 'You can't talk your way out,' he'd say, 'and you can't buy your way out, and you can't shoot your way out, and the only thing that mitigates the matter in the slightest is the fact that nobody else is going to escape. Nobody—no, not one.'"

"I know, I know," said Mr. Hewitt, "but what's the purpose of it?"

"You supported your wife, didn't you?" asked Harry. "You raised a family, didn't you? That's the purpose of it."

"That's no purpose," said Mr. Hewitt. "The same thing that's going to happen to me is going to happen to them."

"The generations have to keep coming along," said Harry. "That's all I know."

"You're put here," said Mr. Hewitt, "and you're allowed to eat and draw breath and go back and forth a few short years, and about the time you get things in shape where you can sit down and enjoy them you wind up in a box in a hole in the ground, and as far as I can see, there's no purpose to it whatsoever. I try to keep from thinking such thoughts, but the last few years almost everything I see reminds me of death and dying, and time passing, and how fast it passes. I drove through Shadyside the other day, and I noticed that some of those factories down there are getting real smoky-looking and patched up and dilapidated, and the thought immediately occured to me, 'I'm older than most of those factories. I remember most of them when they were brand-new, and, good God, look at them now.' And to tell the truth, I'm pretty well patched up myself. I've maybe not had as many operations as some people, but I've had my share. Tonsils, adenoids, appendix, gall bladder, prostate. I wear false teeth, and I've worn them for years— 'your dentures,' my dentist calls them; 'Oh, for God's sake,' I said to him, '*I* know what they are, and *you* know what they are.' And the last time I went to the eye doctor he prescribed two pairs of glasses, one for ordinary use and one for reading, and I can't really see worth a damn out of either one of them. I've got varicose veins from walking around on wet cement floors in Fulton Market all those years, and I have to wear elastic stockings that are hell to get on and hell to get off and don't do a damned bit of good, and I've got fallen arches and I have to wear some kind of patented arch supports that always make me feel as if I'm about to jump, and I've never known the time I didn't have corns—corns and bunions and calluses."

"Oh, come on, Joe," said Harry. "Don't you ever get tired talking about yourself?"

A shocked look appeared on Mr. Hewitt's face. "I wasn't talking about myself, Harry," he said, and his voice sounded surprised and hurt. "I was talking about the purpose of life."

Harry started to say something, and then got up and went out to the galley. It had become too warm, and I went over and opened the window. I put my head out of the window and listened for a few moments to the lapping of the water against the side of the barge. Two of Harry's shad boats moored to stakes in the flats were slowly shifting their positions, and I could see that the tide was beginning to change. I heard the click of the refrigerator door in the galley, and then Harry returned to the bunkroom, bringing four cans of beer. He paused for a moment in front of Mr. Hewitt. "I'm sorry I said that, Joe," he said. "I was just trying to get your mind on something else." Then he stood the cans on the bunkroom table and started opening them. "As far as I'm concerned," he said, "the purpose of life is to stay alive and to keep on staying alive as long as you possibly can."

(1959)

ABOUT THE AUTHOR

Joseph Mitchell came to New York from North Carolina the day after the 1929 stock market crash. After eight years as a reporter and feature writer at various newspapers he joined the staff of *The New Yorker,* where he remained until his death in 1996 at the age of eighty-seven. His other books include *McSorley's Wonderful Saloon, My Ears Are Bent, Up in the Old Hotel, Old Mr. Flood,* and *Joe Gould's Secret.*